A VISION
OF POWER
AND GLORY

A VISION
OF POWER
AND GLORY

JOHN KEHOE

Zoetic Inc.
Training • Growing • Succeeding

Published by Zoetic Inc.
6370 Chatham Street, West Vancouver, British Columbia
V7W 2E2, Canada

ISBN 0-9697551-1-2

Printed in Canada by Best Book Manufacturers Inc.

To my wife, Sylvia

Contents

Acknowledgements

There are many unseen hands that labour behind the scenes before a book is produced. I would like to take a moment to thank those whose efforts are greatly appreciated. To my editors Ric and Jennifer Beairsto for their invaluable guidance and direction. To Linda Naiman for the front and back cover and the illustrations. To my business manager, Soraya Othman, for coordinating everything and being both a friend and a prod. To Mona Othman for her work on the computer. To the staff at Typeworks, Mary, Julie and Vic for the page layouts. To my wife, Sylvia, for acting as the first editor and being a friend, lover and companion. To my many friends who listened to readings of the book in progress and helped with suggestions. And finally to the Great Mystery. For whatever life this book possesses it is but a reflection of the Great One that exists within. To everyone. Thank you.

PART I

The
Beginning

ONE

♦

The Beginning

Before the earth
and sun and moon
Before the worlds
of men and time
The Great Mystery was.

I am a poet and mystic and it is
through this lens that I see the world. It is also through this
lens that my story will be told.

My story is the story of a journey, a journey unlike any
other, a journey which I have now been on for over twenty
years. The journey I speak of is the journey within.

I wish to share a path with you that leads deep into the
Mystery. This path is one of beauty, personal power and inner peace. And this path I know intimately for I have travelled it. I have become it. Of this path I can speak with
authority.

I desire to speak boldly and from my heart about this

journey, this adventure. I will hold nothing back. I will tell you of the first gate and the voice within. About the hidden kingdom and ways of the great ones of old. About sacred songs, visions and more.

But before I continue let me clear up any misunderstanding that one might have about this journey. The spiritual path is not about religions or dogmas. It is not about finding the one true way. Rather it is simply the wonder of one's own beauty being revealed to oneself. Of discovering inner sources of power and guidance, and following the path your heart shows you. It is about opening ourselves up to the amazing possibilities that life affords us. For there is more here than we can possibly imagine, and all will be greatly rewarded who venture within.

Coming into a fullness of power in a spiritual way will make you a better tennis player, a more passionate lover, a shrewder investor, a smarter business person, a better parent. It will intensify and improve your day-to-day activities in ways that will amaze you. You will discover talents and sources of power within you that you never knew existed, and these will uplift and enrich you. Not only will you personally feel and experience your enhanced power, but everyone who comes in contact with you will experience it too, for you will possess an authentic presence. You will accomplish great things in whatever your calling. You will be at peace with yourself. Quite simply, becoming spiritual is the smartest, most practical thing one can do in one's life. The benefits are enormous and the payoff huge.

However, in saying this I know that no amount of words or promises, no matter how eloquent, will bring you even one small step closer to the spiritual path if you are not ready. One must go to the well of living waters of one's own volition. Mysterious are these ways and each of us hears the call at different times and in different circumstances.

Sometimes it will be a traumatic life situation that shakes us to the core and makes us evaluate what is important to us. Other times there is a great emptiness, a hole within us that no marriage, no amount of money or success can fill, so we look elsewhere. Or perhaps a heightened awareness where our consciousness is momentarily uplifted, and we are shown the possibilities of a life lived within the centre. This is what happened to me twenty years ago when I bathed in the glow of the inner presence, my senses alive, wondering to myself, what is happening to me? I felt myself becoming a part of something infinitely larger. Boundaries expanded and my mind was crystal clear and aware. I now know what this experience was but at the time I simply thrilled in this exalted state, drinking from the sweet inner nectar. Whatever it is that acts as the catalyst, something within us awakens and causes us to search for answers. We feel intuitively within us the presence of other realities beyond our senses, and so the search begins in earnest. Like the salmon which leaves the ocean it has always known as home, mysteriously returning to the stream where it was spawned, so too we set out to find our path.

We set off joyously, but very quickly we lose our way. There are many paths, and this can be confusing. Here I will offer some advice: "To thine own heart be true." Do not be too concerned when you lose your way. If your heart is pure and your desire great you will be led back in the right direction. And always remember when choosing a path that a path is only a path, no more no less. That is all it is. No religion or way is the sole custodian of truth. The light that shines within every man and woman who comes into the world cannot be confined or contained in any one small creed or teaching. It spills out abundantly everywhere to everyone who seeks it. It is written in the night sky and every star in the heavens. It can be heard in the cascading waterfall and in a quiet meadow. It is contained in this book and numerous others. It is in the simple words and deeds of thousands of our brothers and sisters as they open their hearts and help one another.

Each step we take brings us one step closer. When we fall, we pick ourselves up. When we're lost we ask within for guidance. When we're discouraged we remind ourselves that many before us have struggled in the same ways and succeeded.

Opening up your heart and taking one step at a time is the only way that ever was or ever will be. I know because I have made this journey. I have penetrated deep into the Mystery and have come back with truths and secrets to share. I wish you to know the methods, visions and intricacies of such a path. I will speak with candour, without exaggeration, about what this path entails and what you can expect. Some of the things I will share will seem incredulous, almost beyond belief, but this is my experience and to this I will remain true. I will speak to you as a friend, for indeed if this book has found itself in your hands we are sure to become friends through the shared experience of these words.

Let me state clearly that I do not believe I am any greater or lesser than the next man. I am only too aware of my limitations, my failings, my stumblings, my weaknesses. I stand before you in simplicity and honesty. I am not pretending to be anything other than what I am: a man who has made a journey and has a tale to tell.

PART II

The
Vision

ONE

♦

The Vision

Holy, holy, holy
Is the splendour of everything.
And I, a little one
Amidst it all
Laughing, singing
Gawking, dancing
While all around me
The Mystery unfolds.

Strange and wondrous things are happening to me. My consciousness is shifting, expanding. I am changed. I see differently. It is as if my eyes are no longer just my eyes but have become windows to unknown worlds where mysteries are revealed and beauty is beheld in ways I could never have imagined before. Ordinary events have become extraordinary. I am apt to be overcome at the simplest of things.

Yesterday, for example, I watched the branches of a tree cast shadows across our backyard. The branches swayed wildly in the wind, and the shadows of the branches shifted incredibly fast across the ground, scurrying about in reckless, random movements. There was no reason to be moved, and yet I was transfixed. It was the shadows. Something mysterious had happened. They were alive. I mean, really alive. No mere reflections. They took on a life of their own and I watched them dance what seemed to be a sacred, secret dance. It was as if a veil had been lifted and I was privy to something private. Suddenly I saw that all was holy and sacred and all events, no matter how mundane they seemed, were joyously alive and filled with vitality and in tune with deep hidden rhythms.

I watched the shadows, as real as children playing, dance in rapturous joy, with movements of perfect symmetry. Every movement became a worship, and every worship a tribute to the sacredness of everything. And it flowed effortlessly, perfectly before my very eyes.

The sun shone down boldly—it, too, alive in ways I have never experienced. Its golden hue bathed and delighted me, caressed my skin ever so gently. A small bird, curved belly and tiny stick feet, hip-hopped into view and it too became bathed in that golden light.

My ordinary backyard, which I had sat and walked in hundreds of times, became the holy temple of the gods. Time froze and remained still like a stone, though movement somehow continued within this new orb of reality. Eternity entered through my skin, into my bones, and my cells thrilled and vibrated and sang sacred songs long forgotten. My heart opened and made me whole—all this just by my very act of witnessing. It was the witnessing, the being with, the non-separateness, that was the entry to this new world. Such was my feeling.

I wept uncontrollably as I heard a voice within me say, "Behold my glory!" And I beheld the radiant glory of all things. I felt humbled, wretched, poor, inferior, for all was so beautiful and I was not.

And again the voice spoke: "Behold your glory," and suddenly I was lifted up and caressed tenderly. My eyes were washed clean and I saw, much to my amazement, that I too was holy and wondrous. And I beheld myself as magnificent and beautiful, and in this glory I bathed and remained.

There was no separateness. All was one and I was one with the all. Boundaries that were never there, though I had thought them to be, came tumbling down exposed and laughing. And I laughed too. We laughed together. Conversed. Witnessed each other as one. Shared our most private intimacies. Became lovers. Swallowed one another. Fused and became lost.

Oh holy moment of nowness come alive, awakened from slumber, where have you been all these years? What shabby life have I been living? What is happening? Oh splendid moment of nowness, revealing everything. Suddenly naked. Alive. Playful. Full of innocence. Wanting nothing. Needing nothing. Desiring nothing. Yet containing everything. Free and joyous. Let me suck you deeply.

And I sucked and drank deeply from the well of everything. And I became intoxicated and wandered aimlessly about, perceiving magnificence in everything I saw and touched.

I do not know how long I remained in this state, but the sun had disappeared when I finally returned to the house.

Not knowing or understanding what was happening, but feeling pure and free and blessed, I lay on my bed. I fell into a deep sleep. Dreams came to me and I was shown truths long forgotten by our race.

Why am I so surprised that these things are now happening to me? Is this not what I'd worked for? Prayed for? Do we not reap what we sow?

The ploughman whose callused shoulder has borne the weight of his plough as he toiled in the hot burning sun expects the earth to respond, or else his work is in vain. Seeds planted, tended, nourished diligently, will sprout and bear fruit in due season. This we know. Yet here I am surprised that this is happening to me.

Nor has it magically happened overnight. Gradually now for several years I've seen changes within myself. Little things, like deeper understanding here, more compassion there. An opening of the heart, the senses becoming more acute. And then there were those delicious moments of oneness with the Great Mystery which came so unannounced, and lingered secretly like an intimate lover, only to disappear again just as unexplained. These were surely signs that the seeds so diligently sown and patiently nourished through years of inner work were beginning to flower within me.

Yet nothing can prepare one for one's whole world to be turned upside down, and for visions of grandeur and beauty to flood the senses with such clarity and intensity as it did yesterday.

I have awakened to something, this much is sure. Awakened to what, I am not so sure. Everything is now becoming different, and yet nothing really has changed. I am confused yet strangely at peace. I feel like laughing hysterically. Is this what the mystics have been hinting and talking about? Is this some sort of enlightenment, or am I deceiving myself? What is going on?

Ours is a great race. A noble race. We are holy and wondrous. All power is given to us. And this truth is encoded deep within us for each of us to discover. We are kings and queens with cosmic royal blood lines, and we have been born with great destinies to fulfil, and we will rule in glory and power.

Our kingdom stretches as far as our mortal eyes can see. It contains mountains and oceans and great forests and waterfalls and surging rivers and rolling plains and the stars and the sun and the moon. It contains inner worlds and dimensions where intrepid travellers, ancient inner mariners, mystics and shamans have travelled and brought back tales of wonder. This too is part of our kingdom. We are greater than our thoughts can imagine. More beautiful than anything our eyes can behold. Such is our glory.

But woe are we. For ours is a kingdom in disarray. A fallen kingdom. A spell has been cast and our race in mortal sleep knows not its truth. We have been tricked into believing a lie and we are paying greatly for it. For we who walk this planet, we who carry the torch of consciousness, we have within us the mark of this lie. It shadows us like a curse. It has hardened our hearts and dimmed our senses and made us into something we do not understand. And this is the tragedy of our times.

How has this happened to such a great and noble race? What trickery is at work here?

Spinning. Spinning. The web of illusion is forever spinning and few are they who remain unsnared. The truth and the lie lay together side by side, and many will be fooled. For the kiss of both is sweet, and both beckon to us. But hear me well and listen carefully to my words.

The lie is not the truth and the truth is not the lie. You cannot wed both. Each of us is given the choice and each of us chooses. Once we have chosen, the choice becomes us and we become the choice. This is the law. Holy is the law. Great is the law.

Those who choose the truth will call it truth, and they will walk in the light. Those who choose the lie will not know they are choosing the lie (for no one chooses the lie knowingly), so they too will call it truth. But they will walk in darkness. Each truth is a lie to the other, and so there is much confusion and dissension among our people.

The ways back to the kingdom are strange and mysterious, not of this world, or so the myths and legends of our race tell us. Some say the kingdom does not exist, that it is only a fantasy, an illusion, and maybe they are right. Each of us chooses. But care not what others say. What do *you* say? What does your heart say? And most importantly, what do your actions say?

What paths do you tread? By what star do you navigate? These are questions we must ask. For if we do not ask them of ourselves, life will surely ask them of us. The lion and the lamb sleep not together. Where is your allegiance?

Our life is a tale being told. A book whose open pages reveal our past and whose chapters to come have yet to be written. An odyssey, an adventure, this drama is real. Embrace it eagerly, for it has embraced you.

Awaken from your slumber, little ones; the kingdom is at hand if you so choose. Nature is on our side. It is an ally. Though sharp of claw and long of tooth it can be wooed. I will show you how. There is light in every corner and crack of the universe. Not even our ignorance can keep it from us.

The tides may ebb and flow. Storms may rage. The night may frighten you with its blackness, but the shores of all you desire are within your grasp if you can believe. But spring smartly—there's much work to be done. This is not the way of the sluggard or the faint of heart. Trim your sails, hearty sailors, we're off on a voyage. Raise yourselves up for the challenge. Do you like adventure? There is adventure aplenty here.

Come, the time is right. Now is the time. Now is the gate through which we must pass. Now is the sturdy vessel we sail. It will faithfully take us where we want to go. Tarry not, your destiny awaits. Grab hold of the tiller and chart yourself a course. Be bold and courageous—it is within you. Navigate skilfully. For this very task were you born.

And if you are sincere and your heart is pure, if you choose well and follow your choice wherever it leads, you will find the kingdom. For this, too, is the law. Holy is the law. Great is the law.

TWO

Honouring the Ancestors

First you must awaken
From the dream within the dream
Then the sacred songs will be sung
This is what the ancestors say.

Buddha was my great-great-grandfather. Christ my second cousin. Mohammed my uncle. I come from a royal heritage. Greatness abounds in my family and I am proud of this greatness. I am proud of my family.

We the human beings are all one. We are one tribe. One family. We share the same cosmic destinies. We walk the same planet. We have the same relatives. And to know this is good.

We who live today have received the outflow and benefit of every spiritual act from every individual who has ever walked on this planet. And for this we should be forever grateful.

Christ died for my sins. Buddha become enlightened so I, too, could become enlightened. Mohammed discovered the truth so I, too, could have the truth. Black Elk had visions so I could share his visions. Every man and woman who has lived and died before me and struggled to find the truth has done so in order that I might benefit. To each and every one of them I owe a debt of gratitude. Their struggle and victories, no matter how small, have not been in vain. My consciousness is richer for their existence.

The river of consciousness which flows through me has existed since the beginning of time. It flows through the minds of all the human beings. The same river flowed through the minds of our ancestors. It is through this consciousness that we raise ourselves up. It is through this consciousness that we are lifted up by the work of others. It is through this consciousness that others are lifted up by us. Every act of kindness, every prayer, every spiritual practice has an effect on the whole. We are all in this together. There is no separation. Not even a blade of grass can be cut without the universe quivering.

And here we come to a truth which is little understood. Within this omnipresent consciousness is contained all which has happened to our race since the beginning of time. Every act and thought has left its mark. Greater ones than we have made inner journeys and they have left a trail. It is easier for us today because of those who have gone before. Not just because of the rich and detailed teachings they have left us, but because the spiritual archetypes created by the ancient mariners, the mystics and shamans who sought the truth within, are forever within us in these inner realms. They burn like brilliant torches and show us the way home. They are beacons for us to follow. Paths already forged. This territory has been well explored, and detailed maps exist for those who wish to follow.

I have heard the ancestors wailing from the great beyond. They call us 'shadows,' we who are alive today. We who have bodies and lives and minds and possibilities—they call us shadows. Why? Because we have no depth. No substance. We have rejected the traditions, gone off blindly on our own without first steeping ourselves in the wisdom of our race. We feel we have no use for their teachings. This mocks the ancestors. We will never find the path of wisdom this way.

We honour the ancestors by studying diligently the paths they walked, by accepting humbly and graciously this gift they have left us. It is sheer arrogance and ignorance to dismiss outright such rich and diverse traditions as outdated and not suitable for today's living. This is the folly of our generation. We feel we have nothing to learn here. Nowhere to get answers. That the spiritual heritages left to us are dead and lifeless. Dead and lifeless? Why these traditions are bursting with truth and wisdom and answers, if we will but take the time to find them. Drink deeply from these sources and steep yourself well in these truths, lest you venture off blindly and get lost in the wilderness. These truths will fill you. They will make you whole. This is milk from the mother's breast. This is manna for those who starve in the desert. Our ancestors were weaned on this, and they grew strong and ventured into the unknown and came back to share their visions. The truth and wisdom of the ages are contained here. We who desire to walk new paths must honour the ancestors before we forge off on our own.

I am not a Christian but the Bible has been a rich and wondrous vein of spiritual truths for me, and I am the better for having mined this abundant source and cleaved to me the truths I have uncovered therein.

I am not a Buddhist but the teachings of Buddha, Dōgen and other Zen masters have profoundly influenced me and changed the way I live and view the world.

I am not a North American Indian but I have touched the Great Spirit during sweat lodge ceremonies and felt the presence of the Great Mystery in the rich spiritual teachings of the Indian people. I have danced sacred dances and learned the wisdom of the sacred hoop and the four ways. I am a better and wiser person for it.

Those of you who thirst for spiritual knowledge, drink heartily. The kegs are full, bursting at the seams—you have merely to help yourself. Who amongst us who hungers and thirsts for spiritual truths could not be filled for a hundred lifetimes with what has been left to us? And still the well would be full. Such is the wonder of our heritage. Look at what diversity and richness our race has produced. You should be proud that our forefathers have accomplished and produced so much. Something for everyone. No one need go away empty-handed.

What is it you want? Ask whatever questions you wish of the ancestors and you will receive answers. For not only do these truths exist in books and oral traditions, but all truth lives forevermore in our consciousness, and this is our gift from birth. The ancestors will come to you in dreams. They will come themselves, or they will speak to the holy messenger and he will come with symbols. You are not alone. Not now nor ever. Within us all truth is alive and waiting for us to discover it. It is so for every human being. We have merely to open ourselves up to it. The field is ripe for harvest. The ancestors have tended the fields diligently. And where do we go to reap this abundance? Go within. Within. Always within. Come, let us fill ourselves.

Honouring the ancestors does not mean following blindly. For they themselves, the great ones, did not follow blindly. Indeed, when closely examined, you will find that they all rejected the spiritual traditions of their day and boldly followed their own vision. They heeded the voice which spoke within them.

Christ was not a Christian. He was a rebel. He abhorred the hypocrisy of the church and its emphasis on dogma and dead creeds. His path was outside of the church. That is not to say one should not be a Christian. If this path has heart and speaks to you then do it with all your being. But do it with a flavour that no one has yet seen. Be a Christian as Christ was and follow the teachings and wisdom of the Holy Spirit that speaks within you. Or be a Buddhist like Buddha. Always look deeply within yourself. Listen to your heart. Listen to your inner voice. In this way you will not be led astray.

Honouring the ancestors means ultimately becoming an ancestor ourselves. Accepting that all is now in our hands. Realizing the torch of consciousness has been passed.

It is now with us. We who are alive on the planet today, we are the new custodians of truth and power. And as such we must claim our own vision. Learn to sing our own sacred song. A song which no one else can sing. And if we fail to discover our song and sing its truth, reveal its beauty, then this song will be lost forever and our tribe will suffer and be the poorer for our neglect. For no one can sing our song but ourselves. It is deep within our heart. Only the awakened heart will release its mystery. No one knows whether your song will be sung. Not even yourself.

I can hear the ancestors. They say, Tell the people to walk proud and sing their sacred songs. The planet needs to be healed. Do you, too, hear this call?

Enough men and women follow the path of pleasure and gain, and this is their right, for all of us choose the path we shall follow. And the path becomes us and we become the path. This is the law of the human beings. But where amongst us are the fire-keepers? The singers of the sacred songs? Those whose prayers and deeds keep the spirit alive?

We must have new legions of men and women in every generation who will accept this challenge, or else the cord will be broken. The earth will grow hard and forget its children. The inner fire must be tended.

Will you be a fire-keeper, a singer of songs? It is not hard—you have merely to open your heart and the rest will happen naturally. Begin by kindling the fire within you so that you become a flame of the Great Mystery. There are gifts that only you can give. Paths that only you can walk. And if you do not awaken these gifts, walk these paths, what then? Then the tribe will be robbed and you will be the thief.

You cannot shirk your responsibility. You think you have nothing to offer? Wake up. Climb out of your weakness. Why if just one person's fire is kindled because of your life, you have done something wonderful. What can you not do when the Holy Spirit works through you? When you have been lifted up. When the sacred holy waters nourish and strengthen you. You are stronger and more wondrous than you imagine. Your sacred song awaits. Your sacred song is your purpose in life. It must be discovered. This you must do for yourself.

Awaken from your slumber. Come, we are together now. The torch is now in our hands. It has already been passed. We carry it this very instant. It is in my hand as I write these words. It is in your hand as you read them. Can you feel its fire? Do not deny the torch is in your hand. You might say, I do not know what to do with it. Or I'm not ready and am unprepared. Or I'm too busy. That's fine. But don't deny it, the torch is now in your hand. Never deny it. To deny it is to be dead to life. To deny it is to be a liar. Do not wait another moment. Life is happening all around us and we are called to participate in a holy, sacred way. This is what the ancestors say.

♦

THREE

Entering the First Gate

Oh web of illusion
Oh spider whose bite hallucinates us
We live in a cocoon of our own making
Wrapping ourselves within our thoughts
These have ensnared us
Mere phantoms of reality
But, oh, how we remain captive in their power.

Let me tell you about the first gate. For until you have entered through the first gate you will not find the kingdom, but will be deceived by the images within your own mind.

We the human beings live as if in a trance. We are hypnotized by the steady, never-ending stream of thoughts within us. Desires, worries, fears, regrets, hopes, fantasies, thoughts of every possible type flow within us. They demand our attention constantly. They overwhelm us. Each of us perceives our world not directly but through these images. They become like a mirror through which we experience our reality. And here is where we are deceived. We live within this maze of thoughts. We live in a cocoon of our own making.

And this is the first challenge that those who walk the path of the human being must confront. How to break out of the cocoon? How to move beyond the stream of thoughts into what lies beyond?

Different spiritual traditions have approached this problem in different ways. The Buddhist will quiet the mind through meditation. The Quaker practices a method called going into the stillness. The North American Indian will chant and drum or perform ceremonies and sacred dances. However, it is not easy to find the first gate amid the clutter of our thoughts, no matter what method you use. Many are they who have searched long and hard and found nothing.

And here I will share with you a secret. Instead of looking for the gate using your mind, let go of your mind and sink into it. Think of your consciousness as a pond of water and sink below the surface as if you were a stone that had been dropped into the water. The stone finds the bottom effortlessly. You will too. Searching with your mind is like swimming on the surface of the water. You could swim all you wish, swim across the entire ocean, and still you would find nothing. You could have the greatest intellect in the world, knowledge enough to fill a library, and still it would remain hidden to you until you learned to let go. Just let go and sink below the surface. When you do this, you will find it.

And what a find! For here we encounter a calmness and peace beyond what we thought possible. We feel as if we are at the very gates of eternity itself. We feel the pulsation of all creation and our intimate relationship with it. We feel a presence. A holy presence? We do not know at first, but a sense of absolute security and assurance overcomes us. Anxieties melt away. And we know beyond any doubt that we are in a special place. And here in this temple within we are nourished and empowered from sources that we neither understand nor desire to understand—so full and complete is the experience. It is enough just to remain motionless without thought or desire, without past or future, without hope or expectation, and bathe quietly in the inner presence.

And here too we find another stream within our consciousness, and this stream is pure and of living waters. And when we drink of these waters we are amazed, for we become strong in spirit.

Within this secret place the inner presence communicates to us, sometimes in words, sometimes with feelings. But always it is there. It tells us we are never alone. Never without its guidance. When it speaks to us it does so as if we were its most favourite.

Sometimes when this presence has invaded me, when I rest sweetly in the inner peace, I feel that I no longer exist but have become part of the living whole. And were all the mysteries of the universe to be revealed to me, they would seem of no value, for what need have I of these things when I have become one with the all?

So sweet is the nectar of this experience when it happens that I neither desire nor encourage the voice to speak but remain like an infant cradled in its mother's arms. Secure. Complete. Fulfilled.

One cannot go through this experience and remain the

same. To know and experience the inner temple and the presence within is to become changed. Let others discuss and argue its existence if they wish. This is of no concern to us. For what was before merely a theory, a hope, an aspiration, now has become utterly real, and our life henceforth is forever determined by this.

"Ask and it shall be given you; seek and ye shall find;... For everyone that asketh receiveth; and he that seeketh findeth; and to him that knocketh it shall be opened."

Once we have been to the inner temple and heard the inner voice, even if only once, even if it is the barest of whispers, these are no longer dead verses. They are living gateways to unimaginable possibilities. Our mind is staggered with the implications. Within us so much more exists.

And well we are to be excited, for within this temple we have merely to listen, to be open and receptive, and all will be revealed to us. I say 'merely' and I smile. The smile of one who has laboured long and hard to woo the voice and understand its ways.

The inner presence seduces us with tenderness and cryptic messages, and then disappears. We must be patient. Resourceful. Alchemy beyond what we understand is at work here, and we must bide our time, however anxious we may be. At first our connection with it is weak, sporadic. Sometimes it is there, sometimes it is not. The threads of connection are very fragile in the beginning. They must be strengthened through familiarity. The inner voice must be wooed. Acknowledged. Praised. Woo it as you would a reluctant lover. Ignore the times it is not there and thank and praise the times it is. Speak to it as if it were a friend, a lover. Establish your own relationship with it in your own way. But never stop praising. Never stop going within. In this way you will become familiar with its ways. Like any relationship, especially a new relationship, you must spend time together. Get to know one another. Does this sound strange?

Sometimes I wonder who is wooing whom. Mostly it is I praising, acknowledging, beckoning to the voice, other times though, it is the one who comes to me. "Where have you been?" it asks when I have too long neglected to go within, for whatever reason. "Come spend time with me." And I do, gladly wondering why I'd ever neglected one so wondrous.

With practice this inner presence becomes a refuge within our busy world. We learn to follow its signals, hunches, feelings when they come. We enjoy going within and being in its presence.

On the surface our day-to-day life remains the same. Difficulties, personal crises, hardships and confusion do not disappear. One still has to earn a living, raise a family and make countless decisions. What does change is our reaction to these things. They no longer seem insurmountable nor even troublesome. Even in the most difficult situations, when we learn to go within, we find poise and guidance in handling them.

Ultimately this kind of living is based on trust. We don't necessarily know from moment to moment how everything is going to turn out. We are never shown the whole picture. Nor do we always have a clear idea of what is expected of us. We take one step at a time. Listening and following.

Once you have discovered this inner sanctuary you will desire to come here often. For when resting here you will feel at peace. From here the inner presence will nourish you. From here you discover that your prayers carry much more power. From here the voice speaks to you sweetly. Helps you in your day-to-day affairs. Tells you truths long forgotten by our race.

To enter freely and often into the land of the first gate is the first victory of the spiritual path. It is cause for much celebration. To the mystics and ancient shamans who have gone before us, it is called the best victory, the most important victory. You have discovered something very great when you have discovered this secret place within you. When one reaches this stage you are indeed on the path.

♦

FOUR

The Book of Law

The Law writes itself within you
And once within you, becomes you
You are the Law
You are the writer

All at once a thousand trumpets blare and the heavens open up and I am lifted and taken to inner realms where the human being goes not. And I am not alone, for the spirits of all the human beings who have lived before are gathered with me.

And before us the Book of Law, as old as time itself, is opened carefully and all are beckoned to come and look within, and there is much amazement for its pages are empty. There is nothing written within.

"Do you know what is real?" asks the voice of Truth to each of the spirits.

And there is a great silence as all ponder the truth as

they have known it, and then like the sound of a raging river I hear the voices of millions, each proclaiming their truth. And each truth is different and there are many contradictions. This I witness. And when the last has spoken, their voices are heard no more. A silence fills the air and there is great expectation.

> *As thou hast believed*
> *So it is true*
> *Whatever you believe within*
> *That you will see without*

So speaks the voice of Truth, then the voice is no more and there is confusion as each wonders the meaning of these words.

Then the spirits are no more and I am alone and in darkness. "As thou hast believed. So it is true," I begin to repeat. And no sooner have these words passed my lips than I am washed in brilliant light. Before me there is a great expanse though I can see it not. The light is blinding, more brilliant than a hundred suns and I cannot see, but neither am I afraid.

"Come to me, little one." The voice of Truth beckons, and I venture timidly for I cannot see and know not where I go. I stumble and fall many times, and each time I pick myself up and continue, following blindly until I hear the voice again.

"Do you know what is real?" it asks.

This time the voice speaks only to me and I hear the words echo far off into the distance, deep into eternity itself. And I realize this is the question that is asked of all who tread the path of the human being. Yet I have no answer within me.

Naked and unashamed, I stand in the blinding light. I feel pure and holy, but no answer passes my lips for I have resolved that no words will I speak until I gaze into the face of Truth directly.

Then I hear a voice within me, and it tells me that one does not see the face of Truth until one has passed through the first gate. It whispers words of truth and tells me what to say. "These are words of power and they will serve you well. With these words you will find your path," I am told.

I repeat the words and all at once the blinding light changes into brilliant colours, like a prism exploding, and I perceive a dawning unlike any I have seen before. More beautiful than anything my mortal eyes have perceived. It is the dawning of my own self, and it happens in the stillness and quiet, and no one witnesses. But I witness and am in awe.

Now I can see far in the distance, and I see a thousand paths all leading to the horizon. Each path is different, and each path has joys and sorrows, pleasure and pain, but some are more beautiful than others. "These are the paths of the human beings," the voice says within me. And I see that each path has a gate and a gate-keeper. And no one may enter unless the gate-keeper allows them to do so.

The gate-keepers chant a sacred incantation, and it is as if the whole universe vibrates to their sounds. And their words sear me like a burning ember, for in unison a thousand voices chant, "What do you believe? What do you believe? What do you believe?" as they have for all eternity and will forevermore. And each human being must answer before he or she is allowed to enter.

I repeat the words of power the voice within me spoke: "All power belongs to those who believe." All at once all paths vanish except for one, and the gate is opened and I walk within.

♦

FIVE

The Temple Within

Prepare thyself, oh little one
Prepare thyself as a bride to the bridegroom
Build me a temple
And worship me within this temple
Build me a temple
Untouched by human hands.

Having mastered entry into the place of stillness within, learning to successfully drop below the stream of consciousness to the place of no thought; having drunk heartily from the living waters and grown strong, I see that this is not enough. I see that more is required if I wish to find the kingdom. And so I pray that the ways will be revealed to me. I pray with faith that I will receive an answer. I pray with the strength of one who has been nurtured with living waters. I pray from the place where prayer carries much power. Then one day while resting in the place of peace I hear these words:

Tarry not, your temple is in disarray
There is work to be done
A new temple must be built
I will show you what to do.

And so I am shown what to do. I am to build the temple within. I am to begin a new life. A life devoted to the temple. I am called to be both labourer and architect. To create a place of beauty within and adorn it with the finest materials I can find. To dwell within and worship and serve my Beloved. For I now recognize the presence within me to be the Holy One. The Great Mystery. The one who has existed before time itself. And so everything changes.

Oh how dull and empty my old life now seems in light of the new vision of the inner temple and what lies ahead. What adventure. What possibilities. Yet I am sobered by the immensity of the undertaking. What is being called for is no less than a complete restructuring of my belief system. I am called to build a temple with new, more powerful spiritual beliefs. To make it strong. My old, limiting beliefs must be changed. There is much work to be done.

I now realize that every belief I possess about myself and my world must be re-examined in this new light. Even my most cherished and deeply held beliefs (especially these!) must be examined, and they must prove their worth before they gain admittance to the new temple. Many will now not fit. Many will be found wanting, inferior. Nothing can be accepted without the closest scrutiny.

Henceforth I decide that no belief, no matter how valid

or real it appears to my mind, will be allowed a place in the new temple unless it will strengthen the temple and make it strong. Will this belief empower me? Will it awaken within me my sacred song? Does this belief assist or hinder me on my path? Each belief must answer these questions. Must account for itself. Must stand naked and reveal itself. Must speak truthfully. Are ye friend or foe?

And here is where the warrior within is called upon to assist. He carries with him a sword and he is ruthless. Nothing is spared. This is a time of turbulence. A time of death and rebirth. A time of transformation.

Each living thing has within it the warrior. You see it in action as the lioness fiercely defends her cubs against hungry predators. You see it as an ant methodically drags an object three times its size back to the nest. It is action and dedication without compromise. Each of us has this within us. It may be called upon for any purpose. And so I awaken it within me.

Some beliefs will argue very convincingly that though they do not help us, in fact hinder us with their weakness, they nonetheless deserve admittance by the very nature of their reality. "We are real and therefore demand admittance," they will say. They will use such logic and trickery to gain admittance, and many warriors are fooled by them. But if the warrior is true to his mandate, these beliefs will be halved and quartered on the spot and will not find entry into the new temple. It is the warrior's task to guard diligently lest inferior materials defile the temple. "Do you serve my master?" the warrior asks of each belief, and each belief must answer, and each answer must be examined carefully. Much will be revealed in this way and many closely held beliefs will be rejected.

Through countless generations of neglect, the stream of consciousness of our race has been polluted by fear, doubt and weakness, and this has given birth to numerous limiting beliefs. Like leeches they suck the life force from us. Blind us to our true power and glory. Oh spider whose bite hallucinates us. Mother of all illusion. Filthy yellow two-headed dog talking out of both mouths at the same time. Liar. Deceiver. Robber. You belong not in the temple.

These beliefs are the wounds that my generation carries, and we bleed and suffer because of these wounds. These are wounds that each of us must heal so that we can become whole.

This is not some simple intellectual exercise. This is the work of a magus. A craftsman. A visionary. Our future will unfold according to the success or failure of this venture. Our destiny will be determined both by the beliefs we hold and those we reject. Whatever we wed within us, this will we become. Whatever we omit from the temple, will be omitted from our lives. This is the law. Holy is the law. Great is the law.

I am prepared to deny my reality. Deny my senses. Turn heaven and earth upside down if that's what it takes to build a temple worthy of this calling. This temple is mine to create. No one can defile it unless I so allow. The temple is mine to mould and fashion and build in the way I choose. I need not accept what others have previously accepted. I need follow no one's vision but my own. I need only be true to myself and the voice that speaks within me.

Oh! The ecstasy of the vision of the temple within. Here I will live. Here I will touch the Great Mystery. From here I will venture into unknown realms. It will be my tabernacle and my chalice. It will be a vessel. And this vessel will be strong, able to withstand the most vigorous journeys, for I intend to explore and explore extensively. I will sail the stream of consciousness into unknown waters. Much awaits me.

My world is opening up. My vision clear. And within me the voice speaks: "Be bold. Tarry not. Build me a temple and I will dwell with you and bring you great treasures." Now I see and understand that there is nothing I cannot do. Nowhere I cannot go. And so it has been, is now, and will be forevermore for the human beings. Great and noble are the destinies awaiting those who dare to follow this path.

SIX

◆

Building the Temple

Sow the truth
Deep within your being
Like a seed it will grow
Fresh shoots will appear
Then you will see blooms
Then the birds will come and sing

The next few months are a period of reflection. A period of introspection. A period of turmoil and confusion. Much the same as living in a house while renovation is taking place. Everything seems out of place and in chaos. A number of limiting beliefs have been rejected outright. Some leave voluntarily. Others need to be dragged out kicking and screaming, time and time again. I think they've gone, that I've swept myself clean of them, only to find them back again a week later, or sometimes even an hour later.

New beliefs are adopted. Some feel right at home and adapt quickly. Others have to be coaxed in and brought back time and time again because they flee when I'm not looking. It is harder than I anticipated. Often I feel like giving up. Is it worth it? I ask myself. But always the voice within encourages me to continue.

Changing from one model of reality to another takes time and patience. It seems strange. Unreal. Often counterproductive. This period of transition stirs up fears, anxiety, complications. I wish I could say it was a smooth transition but it's not. I mention this only so that those who wish to follow will better understand the terrain they will be walking upon. This is not a path for the faint-hearted or the sluggard. Much is required before anything is gained. Those looking for quick results soon abandon this path, calling it a path for fools. But they are the fools, for there is no other way for the temple to be built but by one stone upon another. It is through inner sweat and toil that the temple is raised.

In building my temple I draw from many sources. I drink deeply from the well of my ancestors. Owing no allegiance to any one system I choose the finest beliefs I can find. Beliefs that speak to my heart. I feel no restraints or taboos in borrowing, adding or deleting from one system to the next as suits my purpose. Those who choose to differ with me on this approach have every right to do so if that is their belief. To thine own self be true.

I begin with the biblical quotation, "It is the Father's good pleasure to give you all that you desire."

I begin with this belief because it contains several empowering keys which I can use. First, the Father, God, the Provider, the Great Holy One. Something beyond me exists.

Something referred to as God. And they call him 'my Father.' I have a connection to him. An intimate connection it seems. And it is his good pleasure to give me all that I desire? It is a very powerful belief... if you can believe it.

And so the work begins. I encourage my mind to linger on this statement. To think about it. What does it mean? Who is this Father? Give me all that I desire? It sounds incredulous. Too good to be true and yet there it is in the Bible. It comes from my ancestors. Do I believe it? It doesn't matter. It doesn't matter? I can hardly believe what I am saying.

All at once a shiver runs up and down my spine. I feel as excited as a child who has just taken his first few steps and thus discovered his freedom. Who sees the horizons and possibilities opening up and knows he will no longer be confined. It doesn't matter whether I believe it or not. It doesn't matter!

How wonderful. How free. How exhilarating. Henceforth all my beliefs will be chosen from within and not imposed from without. I will decide what they will be. It will be my choice what I believe. I will create my world from my vision within, not from my senses without. Do I choose to believe it? That is the only question I need ever ask or will ever ask. Would it beautify the temple? Would it strengthen the foundation? Would this be a valuable belief to have in my consciousness? These are the only questions I need ask myself.

So I set for myself a daily program to focus and meditate upon the things I wish to believe. To imprint these into my consciousness much the same way as the multiplication table has been imprinted into my mind, through countless repetitions. I know that any thought or concept which is fed and nourished through repetition will take hold within me. Eventually, if I persist, it will come alive within me. This I know from past experience, so I go to work diligently.

"It is the Father's good pleasure to give me all that I desire." The Father? What is the Father? I imagine a loving, generous, caring God, only God is not right. Doesn't feel right. It has too many religious connotations. Too much baggage. Rather, I imagine the universe unfolding in a generous, loving way. Yes, this feels better. And it pleases the universe to give me the things I desire. I somehow have a connection to the universe. To the Great Mystery. I like this term. It means I need not know exactly what it is. It is great and it is a mystery. This is sufficient for me. I am comfortable with not knowing. It is thrilling enough to know that something so wonderful exists without having to know exactly what it is. If I'm to know more I will be told more, of this I'm sure. And so the Great Mystery effortlessly brings me the things I desire. It is its pleasure to do so. It wants to do so. Incredible!

There is a scripture in the Koran: "When one takes one step towards Allah, Allah takes two steps towards you." It is a similar principle to that of the prodigal son. All will be greatly rewarded who take this path. I like that. I desire that this too be part of my temple.

I will now expect results from this inner work. I will look for them. Acknowledge them whenever and wherever they happen to me. Praise the Great Mystery for its generosity. Rewards, favours, gifts, treasures and more will be given to me. This path will be a path of great joy and abundance. This is my new belief and I will feed this belief. As I approach the Great Mystery, the Great Mystery comes to me.

Sometimes I meditate upon these discoveries. Think about them. Imagine them to be true. Imagine the implications of them being true. Keep my mind focused on each one for a few moments at a time.

Other times I simply repeat statements to myself. Silent whispers, mantras, affirmations. I feed my mind with the things I wish to believe. Letting not the right hand know what the left hand is doing, I daily follow this practice. "Think not of results," said the Russian mystic Gurdjieff, "just do." There is magic and wonder in working this way.

Each day, like eating and bathing, I spend time on this process. I have set for myself the task of believing these concepts. Introducing and reintroducing them into my mind until they become alive within me. When they become a living, flaming reality, then I will stop and not before. They are of no use to me as dead concepts, as something I/read and think about and forget five minutes later. Never mind hopes, wishes, speculations—I want these truths to be as real to me as my hands and feet. As real as the breath in my lungs. As real as my eyes and the sockets that hold my eyes. As real as each of the hundreds of bones that make up my body. As real as the mystery of my existence. For if it is not as real as this, then it is useless. So I labour to claim this reality. To create this reality.

Training the mind in this way is sometimes enjoyable and exhilarating, for one occasionally gets glimpses of the promise to come. And these glimpses quicken us and thrill us to our very core, however fleeting they may be. It is at these times we know we are on the right track. At other times, however, it is simply tedious and frustrating. Mostly —and you may as well know the truth—it's plain hard work. A commitment is necessary. Will, determination, persistence, vision all play their part. One must muster within oneself all inner resources. This is alchemy in its truest form. This work we do is nothing less than a reprogramming of our neurological circuits, creating within us a new model of reality. Building the temple. The temple untouched by human hands. Creating gold from dross. Working magic. Becoming a mighty one.

Not only will this temple serve ourselves, but it will also help to purify the stream of consciousness of the human tribe. For that which flows through us, flows through others. What flows through one flows through all. We are all fed by the same stream. Each of us purifies or pollutes according to the beliefs and thoughts we carry within. And that is why this work is so vital to our tribe. This is why unseen hands will always come to our aid when we work in this way.

To build a temple of beauty and power is a wonderful calling. It is the way of the adept. The way of the mystic and shaman. Previously these ways have been hidden from us, cloaked in secrecy or robed in religious doctrine. Let us lift the veil, once and for all, for all to see. Let us claim this work back from the religions. Great possibilities for transformation exist here. Let the truth be revealed. All may build their temple according to their own vision. One need not be religious. One need only be of good heart and follow the voice within.

And so I labour to build my temple. I choose empowering beliefs drawn from many sources. I search through what the ancestors have left me and I find much I can use. I give thanks to the ancestors for these truths. Truths which speak to my heart become stones for the temple. I listen to what the inner voice teaches me and this, too, becomes part of the temple. I give thanks to the Great Mystery for what it shows me in secret.

And so it begins. I toil not only for myself but for all people. My heart is pure. My spirit eager. And the temple rises, one stone upon another. One truth upon another. I work joyously and am filled with gratitude, for much is being shown to me.

And week by week, month by month, year by year, powerful spiritual beliefs begin to birth within me. No mere concepts, they come alive within me and bring with them a host of treasures. Gifts of exquisite beauty are laid at my feet. I am treated as a king, as a most favoured one. I am lifted up and shown miraculous things. But the most precious gift of all, the one which I treasure above all others, has happened to me. I have awakened from the dream.

PART III

The
Practice

♦

ONE

Coming Home

Nothing is needed
Nowhere to go.
Come home, little one
Come home.

Coming home means deciding that now is the time where there is no retreat or illusion. It means looking at yourself, your life, your place in the universe with neither hope nor despair. Seeing everything just as it is. Seeing yourself just as you are. Stopping for a moment and just letting go, and this takes courage.

Seeing ourselves as we really are is not easy, nor is it always pleasant. We have spent most of our lives trying to be something different from what we are. To have more money, to be more successful, better looking, smarter, more in shape. Yet in doing this we have fled from ourselves, never taken a stand, never claimed our little piece of the universe, however humble. We have taken no time or opportunity to get to know ourselves and discover our beauty. We have been too frightened of what we might find.

Looking closely at ourselves, stopping time and illusion to find out who we are, takes immense courage. For, in examining ourselves closely, we might find that we are not as successful or beautiful or smart or loving as we thought or hoped. And this is a shock. Looking closely we might find that instead of having it all together we're really quite vulnerable and confused and alone and unsure. But this is good to see and know about ourselves. Why run away from it? It's real. If we're absolutely honest with ourselves, we'll admit we've suspected as much. And that's good too. For this is when we can see ourselves, rather than when we're puffed up all full of ourselves or trying desperately to become something else. Let go of it all. Come home and relax. Pull up a chair and get reacquainted with the you that exists right now. The one you've been avoiding and trying to change. Let go of all that nonsense. It's neurotic and self-defeating. Maybe being who you are is not as bad as you suspected. Maybe and maybe not. How will you know until you take the time to find out? It's a risk, but the alternative is to be constantly running away from yourself. And that's too tiring. Besides, you've been doing that your whole life.

Coming home to ourselves is a wonderful thing. It's a big step. A courageous step. When we get to know and accept ourselves, without illusion, a huge weight is taken off our back. Then we can learn to truly relax and enjoy ourselves. It's while we try desperately to be different from what we are that we get stuck.

With taking a stand comes freedom. A new awareness and appreciation of ourselves develops. We become more tolerant of ourselves and even get to like ourselves, faults and all. We become more tolerant of others too. Others suddenly do not have to match our expectations, share our views, be or live the way we think they should. Now there is more space for diversity, contradictions, differences. In relaxing all expectations of others, we can fully appreciate their differences and uniqueness.

Not needing to be anything but what we are, and others not needing to be anything but what they are, it all becomes so open and easy. Suddenly our old way of judging ourselves and others seems so ludicrous. Things are what they are. As we let go and allow life to just happen, instead of trying to orchestrate it, something wonderful happens. We appreciate everything just for what it is.

Living this way means not only coming home to yourself but coming home to life as well. Just as we've fled from ourselves, we've fled from life too. We've tried to make believe it's something that it's not. We've tried to make it into some utopia where our every wish and dream should be fulfilled. We have this image of what we think life should be, and when it doesn't match our expectations, we get depressed, discouraged, disheartened. We are living an illusion. We want life to be what we think it should be or could be or will be. We're afraid to look at it directly. We're afraid of what we might find. Remember when you were small and growing up and you imagined what it would be like when you were an adult? Well, you're all grown up and this is it!

Life is happy. Life is sad. Life is joy. Life is grief. Life is health. Life is sickness. Life is success. Life is failure. Life is excitement. Life is boredom. Life is achieving your goals. Life is failing at your goals. Life is having friends. Life is being lonely. Life is being confused. Life is being sure.

And it's a wonderful thing, this diversity. Life is what it is, and if you stop and look beyond your illusion of what you think it should be, and really examine it closely, you will find that within this diversity lies tremendous beauty and goodness.

We have a life. We have an existence. We have a body and mind. This is precious. We have free will to choose our thoughts and actions. This is wonderful. We are on a journey. It's exciting and terrifying. Our journey consists of constant ups and downs, hopes and fears, but it is a good journey. That the world is good is not just an arbitrary idea. The world is indeed good because we can experience its goodness. Friendship, a brilliant blue sky, making love, children playing, snowflakes, a sunset, acts of kindness, a good joke, the beach, trees, a hot summer day, a good movie, sleeping in Saturday morning, listening to good music, eating delicious food, helping someone out, sitting in front of the fire on a stormy night. One could go on and on and still be just scratching the surface of the goodness one can experience in any given day of a life.

Coming home to life means that we wake ourselves up and give ourselves a good shake and recognize that goodness doesn't happen to us only now and then. It happens quite regularly, almost constantly if you really look at it. We should feel that it is wonderful to be in this world. How wonderful it is to see yellow and blue, red and black, purple and green. All of these colours are provided for us. We feel hot and cold. We taste sweet and sour. We have these sensations and we deserve them. They are good.

We experience the changing of seasons. We experience night and day, the sun and moon. All this is good and nurturing. But life isn't always good. It isn't always pleasant and enjoyable. No, sometimes it can be downright miserable and unfair, but then that's life too.

Come on home. Let go of any bitterness, disappointment, anxiety or frustration, and let the sun warm your bones.

Maybe there's no caviar, but there's always a hot bowl of soup, and it will nourish you. If it's cold put a sweater on. If it's dark turn some light on. If you're lonely call a friend. If you're sick take some medicine.

Maybe you don't look like a movie star but you're not Frankenstein either. Maybe you don't have as much luck or money or love or health as the next person, but there's still plenty of goodness in the world to fill you up if you allow it. Let go of all illusions and come home. Life is forever happening. It is spilling out abundantly all around you, every minute of every day. Come home and enjoy it.

♦

TWO

Bind Thy Wounds

Bind up thy wounds
Carry thyself with dignity
Behold thyself in glory
Love thyself as I love you
In this way you honour me.
And if the wounds cannot be bound,
Bleed, bleed for me
For this, too, is holy.

Self-love is not vanity. It is as
necessary to our being as air and food. It is our duty to love
and accept ourselves deeply, totally, unconditionally. To
prepare ourselves as a bride for the bridegroom. To heal ourselves of all shame, regret and bitterness. To behold ourselves as special. To see ourselves as something of great
worth. To feel we have a place and role in this universe. To
do less is to deny the task for which we were born.

If we desire to know our dignity and nobility we must
learn to love and appreciate the miracle of what we are this
very moment. Our search for meaning and harmony in the
universe can begin nowhere else but with ourselves. If we

fail at this then we fail at everything. If we succeed then much more is opened to us.

I am looking at the flowering dogwood tree through my window this beautiful spring morning. It is blooming magnificently. I have had my coffee and am preparing to write but there it is, demanding my attention, and I am seduced. Each year it seems to flower more and more gloriously, and this morning it is really putting on a show. I'm just sitting here and enjoying it immensely. I am not examining it minutely for every little flaw, though I'm sure there are some. I do not say this flower is beautiful but this one is so-so, and this one could be bigger and this one is not so nice. Or this branch is too weak, this one too short, this one too long and looks funny, out of place. I do not. I just sit and appreciate it for what it is, enjoying it immensely.

I can sit and enjoy the beauty of the dogwood, but not the beauty of me. What is wrong here? Am I less than the dogwood tree? What is this neurotic self-examination, fault-finding, nit-picking feeling going on inside me that makes me feel ashamed, not good enough, unworthy, inferior? Why must I be anything else than what I am?

All at once writing seems to be unimportant to me this morning. This has got me thinking. I have an important decision to make. Am I not as beautiful as any star in the galaxy? As unique as the storm that raged through the night several days ago? As brilliant and radiant as the dawn of a new day?

I ask myself: Is the dogwood tree beautiful or not? I answer, Yes, it is beautiful. Now I'm excited, for I resolve to ask myself the same question. Either I am beautiful, special and unique, or I am not—which is it? There will be no in-between. No safe middle ground. One cannot have two lovers and be devoted to both. Not the lukewarm, pathetic, "part of me is beautiful and part of me is not." Not the neurotic, "I will be fine as soon as I change, become better, lose weight, make more money...."

I will not compromise. I cannot compromise. For the compromise will spew itself back upon me, this I can see. No, the decision must be answered one way or another and it begs to be answered today, now, this very instant. Either I am beautiful, special, unique, or I am not. Which is it?

There are defining moments in one's life when a decision is made, and from that decision there is no retreat. I have boxed myself in and now there is no way out. Now I can go neither forward nor backward till I have answered. And so I answer. I answer boldly. I surprise myself with my boldness, for it is not a timid answer but one of assurance and certainty. I am beautiful, special and unique. I am. And having claimed it, I suddenly see it is true. I see it now clearly, not with my intellect or reason, but with depth and assurance. I feel it deep within my being, as if I'd known it all my life.

Suddenly all is radiant. Is that the dogwood tree smiling back at me as if to say, "What took you so long?" Are the birds grinning at me? Have I suddenly been initiated into some secret? All at once a huge weight seems to have lifted and I feel free and light.

♦

Let me speak of wounds and scars, for it is time that we love ourselves deeply. An unsavoury, emotionally charged incident can produce in five minutes shame that lasts for forty years. Shame is the name we give to the sense that we are unworthy and inadequate human beings. It is a crippling condition, all too common, and belongs not with those who desire to walk the path of beauty.

A marriage breaks up. You lose your job and are unable to find a new one. A lover or close friend mocks you. You put on weight and look at yourself in the mirror and don't like what you see. You fail at something that was very important to you. You let someone down badly. Someone lets you down badly. Our journey through life includes such things. We will fail as well as succeed. And we will have times when we're wounded internally, of this you can be sure. Battle scars, I like to call them. But wounds are meant to be healed and we can be stronger for them. There need be no shame in failing or being wounded. One's life is an epic odyssey. Battles won and lost. Opportunities missed and seized. Fortune and misfortune both ours to experience.

If you have no scars, no time you've battled shame, no bitter regrets or humiliating failures, then what kind of life have you been living? You are not of my tribe and belong not at my table. I sup with those who have failed as well as succeeded, whose battle scars cover their bodies and who are proud to have lived and lived gloriously, through all that life has offered. Those that have bound their wounds and moved on.

But shame that festers will not heal, and here we must be vigilant. Such shame tears and wounds the psyche, as if one had swallowed barbed wire, and your every movement feels its presence. Even going to the corner store to buy groceries can be an ordeal when we are so wounded, let alone feeling alive and free.

And so I set out on a journey to bind my wounds and rediscover my wholeness. But what of my faults, my inadequacies, what of them, for they are there? I resolve to love them. To accept them as a part of who I am. To believe I am beautiful not in spite of them but because of them. They are part of my uniqueness, like markings on a wild animal. They give me flavour. They make me real.

Wounds heal when we forgive ourselves and others for our humanness. We allow ourselves and others to fail and make mistakes, to not be perfect. We forgive ourselves for lost opportunities, foolish decisions. We forgive ourselves for all our past and future errors. We recognize our vulnerability and fragility, and, far from being a weakness, we see this as part of who we are. Our quirks and idiosyncrasies, all part of our distinctiveness. We are special and beautiful because of our humanness, not in spite of it. In fact this is where our true beauty lies.

And let us not complain bitterly every time we are wounded. Let us see the gifts that wounds bring. They spur us, change us, give us compassion for ourselves and others. They renew us as a spring rain. They add to us immeasurably. We are the better for them. And besides, wounds heal.

But if the wound will not heal, what then? Then let it bleed. Let it bleed and soak the earth in its pain and sorrow. But let there be no pity or bitterness. If you can do this then your pain will become an offering, a cleansing, and the greater whole will benefit and be nourished. Offer it joyously. Everyone must at one time or another carry a burden. No one is immune. It is the law of our being. And some carry greater loads than others—this too is law. Ours is not to understand but to walk the path we find ourselves upon.

Conscious suffering brings its own joys and rewards. There are secrets that are revealed here and nowhere else. If we have done everything humanly possible to rectify the matter, worked and toiled the fields. If we have prayed for guidance and listened sincerely and followed the guidance. If we have purified ourselves of all self-pity, depression, anger or resentment. If we have done all this and our path leads still further into the valley of sorrow, then brace yourself for the journey. Lift the cup to your lips and drink. 'Not my will but thine' becomes our mantra, and we venture ahead fearlessly, knowing there are gifts and treasures on this path too.

A wound untainted with pity or bitterness brings the blessing of deep compassion and understanding. We see the human condition, ourselves included, and we feel the pain and suffering of others deep within us. Suddenly we see hundreds, thousands, worse off than ourselves, and all the time we thought our suffering was great. Now we feel ashamed, for we see we are blessed.

The wound becomes a new window through which we see the world reborn, and, released from self-absorption, we marvel at what joys and wonders we now see. A friend coming over to visit, the smell of fresh flowers, the sound of rain on the roof, these things touch and bless us deeply. Paradoxically life becomes more rewarding and not less during these times, and we wonder why we ever worried over such trivial matters in the past, and we thank the universe for our present blessings.

But if the unhealed wound is tainted with self-pity, anger, resentment, bitterness, then indeed we walk through the very paths of hell, and great is our anguish. Inner demons torment us, ridicule us, defile us, and our sorrow swallows us up. All becomes ugly, and the sun and moon and all things beautiful are hidden from us, and there are no treasures or joys on this path, for it is the path of blackness and death.

But always there is a way out, and always the path is through ourselves. Great and holy is the Mystery that shows us these things and teaches us the way to the light.

THREE

♦

Judge Thyself Not

Judge thyself not too harshly
Little ones, lest thy judgment
Becomes the Truth and the Law
And fasten itself upon thy neck
And hang there like a stone.

The Great Mystery never judges
me. It supports, nourishes, loves and accepts me totally.
And it encourages me to do the same. "Love thyself as I love
you," it whispers in my ear.

And it is not just me the Great Mystery loves. It com-
forts everyone, even the most wicked. Such is its love. None
will be punished except those who punish themselves. All is
forgiven when you forgive yourself. One thing and one thing
only is asked of us: that we love and accept ourselves as the
universe has loved and accepted us. That is all.

Now I see that I can do no wrong. If my heart is pure

then all is well. I am of the universe, as pure and wondrous as anything created. All my paths are holy paths by the very act of my treading them. I need not be ashamed of anything.

Henceforth I resolve to renounce all guilt and remorse for all mistakes, past and future. One does one's best. No more is asked. No more expected. Sometimes I will make bad decisions—this I know. Sometimes consequences will result which will hurt people. I am human. It is bound to happen. But I will not pay too much heed to these things. I will offer a silent prayer and move on. I have better things to do than fret. There is no point in regret or self-recrimination. What use are these? For no matter what I think I have done, no matter how dire the consequences I imagine will result from my thoughtlessness, the sun will still shine and the moon will still go through its cycles. In winter it will snow and summer will still be the time to sip cool drinks and put your feet up. Spring will still be the time for lovers, and the first kiss will still be exciting. The mango tree will still produce fruit sweet to eat and the rains will still nourish the soil. Women will still birth children who will grow and birth more children. The stars that dot the sky will still be uncountable. Rivers will still run to the ocean and the tides of the ocean will still ebb and flow. The mighty cedar will still tower high into the heavens and the birds will still sing at dawn. So what is the problem?

The Great Mystery loves us. Supports us. Accepts us. Worships us. Let us not do less. Let us, rather, celebrate ourselves. And when we do this, when we forgive ourselves for all failings, we allow ourselves to be completely human.

Beautifully human. Celebrate our humanness. Celebrate our right to make mistakes. When we open ourselves up in this way and let go of our harsh judgments of ourselves—something wonderful happens within us. We flower, bloom and grow strong in this ever-present love and acceptance. It is oil for our lamp, and as our lamp burns brighter, we are amazed, for we begin to see ourselves as we really are—we see our true worth.

And as we learn to regularly behold ourselves in this way, day by day, week by week, parts of us that were hidden begin to reveal themselves. Talents and gifts we never knew we had divulge themselves to us. And everything becomes bathed in the warm glow of love and acceptance. Unconditional, total, complete love and acceptance is called for. No part of ourselves is to be omitted. Every weakness and inadequacy loved and accepted. Even the dark parts of ourselves loved and accepted. All or nothing—this is the challenge. And when we rise to the challenge, great alchemy takes place.

Like buds on a tree bursting on a warm spring day. Like seeds buried in warm, wet, fertile soil. Like birds singing the glory of a new day, so we too bring our glory into existence with this love. Without it we are dead and barren. Skeletons. Crippled. With it we become everything. All things become new. There is a new dawning. A life without shame or regret. A life filled with love and acceptance. A life nourished from within.

As the ant accepts the ground and the ground accepts the ant. As the night accepts the moon and the moon accepts the night. As the leaf accepts the branch and the branch accepts the leaf. We accept ourselves. And so we become complete and whole and venture further into the Mystery.

♦

FOUR

Prayer

Dance to me, sing to me,
Praise me in all ways.
Let your heart and mind
Be filled with me.
And I will come to you
You will eat at my table
I will serve you
You will become as my most favourite
And all things will I do for you.

Prayer is food for the universe, and it can be prepared in the most creative of ways. Just as a good cook is inventive with food, one can be equally creative with prayer. The possibilities are infinite once you have a feel for it. You will find it immensely enjoyable and richly rewarding. It will nourish you deeply and will supply you with an abundance of all things. The most important thing is not to feel intimidated by prayer. Just as anyone can learn to cook, anyone can learn to pray. A little practice is all it takes.

I love to pray and I'd like to share with you some of my favourite recipes, but first let me tell you a story. Actually, it's a Tolstoy short story concerning a bishop and three hermits.

It seems that while on a voyage sailing towards a particular monastery, a bishop became aware of an isolated island where three hermits lived. Overhearing several pilgrims who were also making the voyage, he learned that the hermits were conducting spiritual practices, and he wished to investigate.

As they approached the island, the bishop asked the captain to anchor while he put to shore with several oarsmen in a smaller boat. Upon arriving and speaking to the hermits, he discovered that they were saying prayers of their own making. Wishing to correct this, the bishop took it upon himself to teach them the proper prayers according to Holy Scripture. They, not realizing that they were doing something wrong, readily agreed.

The hermits were simple men and, being advanced in age, had difficulty in remembering the words of the prayer. All day the bishop had them repeating the words, until all three could finally say them without help.

That evening, as the moon appeared, he returned to the vessel. The sails were unfurled and they sailed away. The bishop watched from the stern as the tiny island disappeared into the distance.

Later that night the bishop saw something white and shining coming from where the island had been. "It must be a boat sailing after us," he thought, but it was overtaking them so rapidly that this seemed unlikely, and he could see no sails.

He called to the helmsman, "What is it?" though already he could make out the three hermits moving across the water, all gleaming white, their grey beards shining as they approached the ship as quickly as though it were not moving. The hermits beckoned the ship to stop. All three were gliding along the water without moving their feet.

"We have forgotten your teachings," they spoke in unison, "teach us again."

"Your own prayer will reach the Lord," replied the bishop, bowing low before the old men in humility, and they turned and went back across the sea. And a light shone until daybreak on the spot where they were lost to sight.

Each of us prays in our own way, and if our heart is pure then it is a good prayer. The spiritual path is a path of prayer. Prayer is food for the soul, for the spirit, for the universe. Prayer is communication. It is the whispers between lovers. It is the silent intimacies between oneself and the Great Mystery. Prayer connects us, humbles us, strengthens us, enlightens us and makes us one with the Great Mystery.

We pray not because it is expected, not because we feel obligated or because some rule or mandate necessitates that we pray. No, we do it because it is joyous communication with our lover. We hunger for the spiritual presence that thrills us to the core.

We receive so much in prayer, not just what prayer brings, which is much, but the grace and presence of the Holy One's company. When the Great Mystery invades us, penetrates us, and we feel ourselves in it and of it, all else melts away. And this is one of my favourite ways to pray. The prayer of the Holy Presence. The prayer of moment-to-moment worship with the Great Mystery. When I am very still, very in tune, I feel the joyous pulsation of creation. I feel it in every cell of my being, and everywhere I look the Great Mystery is there. Wave upon wave of perfect peace and harmony pulsates through me.

Every act is a divine act when my lover so possesses me like this. Every encounter is an encounter with the Holy One that lives within me. Like Walt Whitman, I, too, proclaim:

"I hear and behold God in every object, yet I
understand God not in the least
I see something of God each hour of the
twenty-four, and each moment then,
In the faces of men and women I see God,
And in my own face in the glass
I find letters from God dropped in the street
and every one is signed by God's name.
And I leave them where they are, for I know
that others will punctually come forever and ever."

The prayer of moment-to-moment worship with the Great Mystery. Oh, what a special prayer this is. One needs to spend time alone with the Holy One. Like any relationship it must be built and nurtured. It needs familiarity. Trust. Quiet, special time together. To be with the Great Mystery in such a way is not to simply think about these things. It is beyond thought. Beyond concepts. It is quiet times of prayer and worship. Losing oneself in the presence.

Sometimes amidst the busiest of days, overcome in the details of my life, the Great Mystery comes and visits. Suddenly it is there, and all concern and anxiety melt into non-existence, and I am transcended and uplifted and exist not alone but within divine protection. In these times the completeness of everything is revealed to me, and it is as if I see through my Beloved's eyes, not my own. This is the prayer of the Great Mystery's ever presence.

To pray with a heart full of praise and gratitude is another way of praying that gives me great joy. Each day I say a simple "I love you," perhaps in the morning. Or I say, "Thou art so magnificent and wondrous," when I see something that moves me—the sun breaking through the clouds, a bird arcing in the wind—affirming my love and acknowledgment of the Great Holy One. I never tire of praising. I woo the spirit as a lover. I acknowledge the Great Mystery. Praise it. Appreciate it.

Every meal when I offer grace, a practice which gives me great pleasure, I find something to acknowledge: the pleasures of the day, the company of friends, the success of a venture, my health, the nutrients in the food, the smells—simple everyday pleasures I acknowledge. Every gift, every pleasure, every sight and sound comes from the Great Mystery. I have much to acknowledge and be thankful for. Wherever my eyes gaze I see these treasures. And the more I thank and praise, the more beauty I perceive. It is as if the constant praise somehow washes and cleanses my eyes, so even more is revealed. I have heard mystics report such things and I, too, repeat it. The prayer of praise and gratitude is one of the doors into the path of beauty.

I never miss an opportunity to praise and thank the Great Mystery. I acknowledge it for everything. A sunny day, my health, the people I meet, the successes and joys I experience in day-to-day life. Everything is from the Great Mystery, and whenever I remember to, I make acknowledgment. In this way I feel connected, blessed, special.

If I were to praise the universe a thousand times a day it still would not adequately express my deep appreciation for all that the Great Mystery does for me. For the great joy and privilege of having a life.

If I were to live in eternity, how joyful it would be to join the holy celestial choir and sing and praise the Holy One for ten thousand years or more.

"Holy, holy, holy art thou Oh Great One," my voice would echo to the far reaches of the universe. How thrilled I would be to participate in honouring its Greatness, singing its glory. I have felt the Great Mystery and witnessed its good. I know firsthand how all encompassing its beauty and love, how nurturing its touch, how complete its forgiveness. What a small, simple thing it would be to participate in its glory this way. I have imagined such things in my mind. And sweet are these thoughts, for they nourish me deeply.

The prayer of love and acceptance is the practice of loving and accepting as the Great Mystery loves and accepts. I start with myself. I love and accept myself totally, for I know that until I can do this I cannot truly love another, not even the Great Mystery. I must fully acknowledge, appreciate, worship at the temple of my own unfolding.

When I ridicule, degrade, put myself down in word or thought, then I ridicule the work of the Great Mystery. With every shameful thought of myself I shame it. And not wishing to cause shame I lift myself up. How ironic it is that in its glory I glorify myself.

Next I love and accept my fellow brothers and sisters, those who walk the planet with me, even the ones who are most annoying or repugnant to me. Especially these, for there is no great accomplishment for me or the Great Mystery in picking and choosing whom I will love and whom I will not. In holding those close to me whom I agree with and admire, and condemning those whom I oppose. What good is this? Even those who have perpetrated crimes against my brothers and sisters and have showed no remorse, must we not love these people as well?

How deep is our love if we cannot love the violator as well as those being violated? The perpetrator as well as the victim. Do not both urgently need love and healing? Was not the command to return love for hate, good for evil? And if we cannot do this, can we have it as our ideal? Can we at least sometimes extend ourselves beyond our normal ways of relating to people? Can we become less judging and more loving? Is this not one of the ways of awakening our heart, so that the Great Mystery can live within us?

A good friend told me about witnessing an animal rights demonstration where one of the activists, upon seeing a woman in a fur coat, charged towards her in fury. So intent was he on confronting her that he stepped on several homeless people who were lying on the sidewalk, and he continued on without apologizing or seeing how they were,

lest the woman wearing the coat escape without his chal-
lenging her. So intent was he in his pursuit that he failed to
see what was right in front of him. We must guard that the
same does not happen with us. Righteous indignation is a
frightful thing. Too often we become righteous, know-it-all,
when we think we have all the answers. When our way is
the only way. We become judge and jury. But that is not
what we are called to do. Let the Great Mystery do the judging, let us do the loving. This is our call.

If we work for social change—and it is good to do such
things—let us always do it with an awakened heart big
enough for all. There is no enemy; there is only ignorance.
There is no one to hate, only many to love.

When I find that I have difficulty accepting, condon-
ing, loving a person because of some righteous reasons I
have constructed in my mind, I ask myself, "Does the Great
Mystery love this person?" And always the answer is yes.
Should I then do less?

Deep within each of us there is a flame that burns, and
that flame is the spark of the Holy One. In some it burns
brightly, in others it is barely distinguishable, but always it
is there. With love and acceptance this flame grows. We can
help others to kindle this flame by seeing the good in them,
even if they don't see it themselves. Especially then, for this
is the work of transformation, and great is this work. And
blessed are those whose awakened heart allows them to do
such healing work. Without such labourers the fields would
indeed be barren. These are the fire-keepers and great is
their calling. Great is their glory.

Also in prayer, I love and accept my life, imperfect as it

is. For it is the one I am living. It is the one I have been given. No matter how much I might wish it were different, it is the one I have. My life is holy, sacred and special, of this I am certain. If I cannot see this, then here is where my work begins. This life of mine is a miracle. A sacrament. It is a great honour, a great privilege to have this experience of life. Every day I give thanks and praise for this honour.

And finally I love and accept the Great Mystery. Paradoxically, I find that when I pray in this order I am most aware and in tune. If I begin by loving and accepting the Great Mystery, which is of no difficulty at all, I might find that I do not accept my brothers and sisters, or myself. The Great Mystery is worthy but these others are not, I reason. But if I must go the other way to get to the Great Mystery, if I must love first myself, then my brothers and sisters, and then my life before I deserve the right to worship the Great Mystery; if these are the gates I must pass through to be with it, then I make the effort, because of my love for the Holy One.

These are simple prayers but powerful prayers, and they flow from my heart and mind all day, every day, and they bless and nurture me deeply.

The prayer of request is what most people think of when they think of prayer: asking for something. It is a very relevant prayer and one that can be used most effectively, but let me share with you a secret. Call it a cooking tip if you will, from one who has created many a feast using this technique. My recipe actually is not my own. I borrowed it from a scripture. I have tried it many times and can attest to its merits:

> *"Whatsoever ye pray for and ask for, believing
> ye have received it, ye will receive it."*

Whenever I want the Great Mystery to bring something into my life, I create that image in my mind. I spend quiet time each day and claim it as mine already. I don't wonder if it will happen. I don't hope or plead. I don't get on my knees and beg. I simply create the images in my mind and live the experience of having it. I live it with feeling and intensity for several moments at a time.

And when I am finished I just let go of it. I don't try to hang on to the feelings and images. I don't force myself to try to believe it every moment all day long—this is not necessary. Let the Great Mystery work with these images in its own way. The power it possesses is greater than my understanding. Always during the prayer I believe that it has already happened to me. This is the secret ingredient. And I continue to pray in this way until I begin to see it happen to me.

I cannot recommend this method too strongly. I have used it with great effect many times in my life. It will nourish and bless you in a variety of ways, and always remember —it is the Father's good pleasure to give you the things that you desire.

Both novice and experienced cook will have great success with this recipe. Use it often or whenever required. Feel free to alter any of the preceding recipes according to your own taste, adding or deleting as necessary. This is what all good cooks do. Put your own imprint on prayer. Do it in your own way.

Pray for others and pray with others. Your husband or wife, the children, friends, fellow-believers. Too often, if we pray at all, we pray only by ourselves. It is so empowering to hear a prayer from someone's heart and to participate silently in it. It doesn't matter whether the words are simple or eloquent—when it comes from the heart, it is a healing balm, and all are nourished who hear it.

How many times in the sweat lodge has my heart been pierced with the simple but honest prayers of my brothers and sisters as they've opened their hearts and prayed from their centre? This is the beauty of shared fellowship. Even if it is with just one other person. We nourish each other deeply with our prayers no matter how humble they are.

Once you have awakened to the joys and pleasures of prayer, you find no difficulty in praying many times every day. You will do it because it empowers you, makes you feel connected, brings you closer to the fire that burns within. For with prayer comes growth, and with growth comes the realization of our oneness with the Great Mystery. Such are the workings of prayer. And so we learn to live in a sacred manner.

♦

FIVE

The Darkness

When darkness engulfs you
Fear not for I am near.
Behold I will give you a lamp and oil
And this will be your light
Keep watch. Be vigilant.
As surely as day follows night
I will return.

Dedication and devotion to the great work must be done again and again. You must rededicate and redevote yourself after the inevitable lapses and periods of dullness and inactivity. And there will be countless of these periods before any true growth or stability appears.

It is too easy to believe when reading the works of the great sages, mystics or shamans that they never had periods of doubt or confusion, or weeks of inactivity, or times when dullness seeped into their consciousness, times when all seemed hopeless.

Writing is a selective process. It is easy to write only of

the ecstasy, the heights, the wonders, and eliminate the dross. Such writing makes for wonderful reading but it is not real, at least it does not depict the whole of reality.

I look at my spiritual journal, which I keep daily, and it is a humbling experience. I find many jewels and much insight, yet I also find, again and again, periods of inactivity, depression, despair, confusion. And when I read these what does it do? It fills me with immense compassion. Compassion for myself. And it fills me with respect for the immensity of the task. Easy, some think, to find the kingdom. Yes, easy in theory. Easy to take the first few steps. Easy to ride the crests of heightened awareness when the tides of consciousness are at their peak. Easy to read the books. Easy to have good intentions.

Anyone who thinks it is easy has not put his shoulder to the plough and worked the fields. Has not stalked the elusive prey through countless cold, black nights, only to lose the tracks and wander aimlessly in the dark. Has not dropped his line into the deep mysterious waters and come up empty time and time again before even the faintest nibble is felt. And here is where a daily journal can help.

The daily spiritual journal is an invaluable tool which the aspirant uses to chart his or her progress and discover the ebbs and flows. Our inner territories must be mapped and explored if we wish to understand and make headway into this mysterious inner terrain.

The daily journal will also humble the seeker, for he will discover how feeble and transitory his best intentions are. With lofty ideals and a steely determination we decide to devote ourselves to various spiritual practices. And with the best of intentions we begin, perhaps with even an air of superiority in our manner. We do this inner work for several days or weeks, but then we start to miss a day or two here and there, and then maybe a week or two, or sometimes even a month or two, until finally we catch ourselves and ask, somewhat amazed, "What happened?"

So we begin again, and this time it will be different, we resolve, this time we will keep to our program, but again we fail and fall. The daily journal allows us to watch our attempts, starts, half starts, our periods of productivity and slackness. Even attempting to keep the daily journal is revealing. At first there is an entry every day, then we miss a few days, and suddenly we go to our journal and three weeks or three months have gone by and nothing has been written. What has happened?

This is work which defies normal understanding. One must never underestimate the immensity of the task. There is more here than meets the eye.

Let the truth be known. You will fail and fail again. You will stumble and fall hundreds, even thousands of times. Before any real growth and stability appears you will despair, lose faith, get discouraged, doubt, feel sorry for yourself, wonder if anything will ever happen.

Does this mean you've lost the path? No, not at all. Here is something valuable to know—this is the path. There is great frustration in the beginning—in the infancy of our dawning spirituality—and it is here where we need patience and dedication. One oscillates between ecstasy and total despair. Ecstasy when through the grace of the Great Mystery the Holy Spirit fills us and we live in full and dazzling awareness of its existence, for it is alive and within us, and this we know. We reign in confidence, inner peace and joy. Truths are revealed and deeper understanding manifests within us.

We experience total despair when just as unexpectedly as it arrived, the awareness leaves again, and we wonder whether we imagined the whole affair. Doubt creeps in and a darkness overcomes us, and we have no lamp or oil and must remain in this state for days, maybe weeks. And we try desperately to regain that feeling, the state of oneness with the Holy One, and all our efforts are in vain for what feels like an eternity. And then suddenly, it returns again.

It will save the aspirant much inner turmoil if you understand that there is an ebb and flow of consciousness, that the inner journey flows with tides just as real as the oceans'. This must be taken into account as you build your inner sanctuary.

I wish I had known this many years ago when I struggled relentlessly to gain the light, only to crash in frustration when it left. I was always asking myself, "Why?... Why did it leave?" thinking it was something inadequate about me, something I was doing wrong. Maybe I wasn't sincere enough? But now I know and understand the tides, and when the darkness comes I have a lamp and oil, and I wait for the light to return. There is calm and assurance. I am an experienced mariner; I have sailed these waters before. I have charted and mapped this territory. I am at peace in the dark.

Spiritual practices done during the darkness are not without benefit. On the contrary, they are necessary parts of the path, and they strengthen our inner being immensely. Without them we would not advance. We should be grateful for these opportunities. If you wish to venture into deep waters, you must learn to swim, not just with the current but against the tide as well. This is not a journey for the timid or frail. Your will and resolve will be tested again and again.

So have an infinite amount of compassion for yourself and your struggles. Pick yourself up again and again. Everything is as it should be.

All things come to those who are dedicated to the path.

♦

SIX

Details

Within the one, many.
Within the many, one.
Everywhere to be found.
Nowhere to be seen.

Paying bills, going to the dentist, cooking meals, making the bed, going to work—a life is full of details. Talking to a friend on the phone, running out to the store to get something you forgot for the evening meal, doing the laundry, ironing your shirt, watching a movie. Details. Mundane details. Yet it is in these details that the fabric of life is revealed. A tapestry so intricately woven. The different threads and colours that blend unobtrusively. The fabric a whole, and yet each thread a part of the whole. Were there no parts, there would be no whole, and so I love and rejoice in the parts because I love the whole.

What is not important in a life? What is to be ignored, hurried past, shunned? What is life if not the details?

Brother Lawrence, the Christian mystic who attained his spirituality through devotion to his duties as a cook in the monastery, said, "God does not measure the size of a deed but the amount of love that goes in it." Brother Lawrence whose simplicity and purity confounded his fellow brothers, who insisted to anyone who chose to listen that prayer time was of no concern to him, for his every act was a prayer. He who was puzzled by the need to go to the chapel during prayer time to pray and offer devotion, since his very life was devotion. He considered this time wasteful; really he should be in the kitchen working and preparing meals for the brothers.

If I can touch the Holy Spirit during prayer and meditation, why not while drying the dishes too? Why not while travelling in my car to an appointment? For if I cannot do it during these times, then what kind of relationship do I have?

Everything becomes magnified when I realize the details are a manifestation of the Holy One, and I am participating in this miracle. Ordinary? Nothing is ordinary unless the most beautiful gem is ordinary. Unless the cry of a newborn child is ordinary. Unless the brilliant colours of a sunset are ordinary. Everything is extraordinary in its own beauty. And even when we forget this, when we panic, despair, feel confused, overwhelmed—is this not, too, part of the details of a life? Are these to be shunned? Or rather embraced, loved, accepted as a part of who we are?

Must every star be the brightest?

Must every flower be the most beautiful flower?

Must every colour be the most brilliant?

If so, where is the contrast, the divergence of hues, the ebb and flow of a life unfolding?

And so my steps are steps of joy. Steps of wonder. Steps of praise and acknowledgment.

I am the miracle and the miracle is all around me.

I am the truth and the truth wraps itself around me.

I am beauty and beauty is everywhere for me to behold.

I am the mystery unfolding and I behold myself and I am in awe.

For I am the weaver and I am the thread. I am the colour orange and yet I am the colour blue. I am the whole and I am the part.

A bird, a stone, the wind, the human being—each of us has our own reality, yet we are all one family. Each living and non-living thing is intimately connected with each other thing. Each has its own song to sing. Each fulfils a purpose. Everything has a destiny.

Everything is part of the tapestry. Every thought and action. Every movement we make, no matter how insignificant we may think it is, is a tiny thread in the whole. Each of us participates in our own way. Each of us adds to the tapestry. Each of us weavers. Together with the sun and moon and every living thing we make the patterns, and so the Mystery unfolds. There is no separation. We are all one. All sacred. Holy, holy, holy is the One who shows me these things.

♦

SEVEN

The Awakened Heart

Breaking out of the prison
Of little self
I find myself
Flowing into everything

The awakened heart exists in one whose boundaries between self and other have been expanded. I would like to say disappeared but that is an exaggeration. For the boundaries do not so much disappear as cease to matter. Casual acquaintances become friends, sometimes even total strangers become family. This happens because our heart has awakened to greater realities. It no longer beats cold and lonely within its own small confines but becomes soft and tender and reaches out to embrace all. This is a great blessing, for it allows us to feel deeply and see the beauty of things that were previously hidden to us.

We feel the loneliness of old people, the confusion and awkwardness of the young, the desperation of the homeless and unemployed, the hopelessness of the alcoholic and drug addict, the fear of those who are sick and dying, the anguish of the divorced couple as they wrestle with their separation, the pain and shame of the criminal.

And so we help. We help because we want to help. Our heart leads us to help. To lend a hand, an ear, give some time, concern, money—whatever seems appropriate. And we find that by doing so we are nourished and empowered and become the greater for it. And as we lose ourselves momentarily in our service to one another, we find a nurturing inner peace.

Unfortunately, our lives are complex, overcrowded, full. Sometimes we feel we are too busy to be of service. There are always so many things we have to do, and they all seem so important to us. But if we do not value and put importance on awakening our heart, helping one another, if we do not see this as an important and invaluable part of our growth and development, what does that say about us? Is our spirituality simply an intellectual exercise? Something we think about or read about in books? What path are we on if service is not part of our journey? Do we really think that making more money, watching another night of TV or going to the tavern will make us happier or more content? Maybe what we really need is to open up and feel deeply our special relationship to life and others. To break out of the prison of constant preoccupation with self. Let more into our narrow world. Open the windows and let in some fresh air. Let our heart breathe and beat for more than just ourselves. When we do this, what healing balm it is to the soul. How we grow and expand with this oil in our lamp.

The gift of our life is an honour, a privilege, a sacrament for which we are forever indebted. The awakened heart never forgets this. Service comes from a profound appreciation of life. We are blessed with riches and joys innumerable, no matter how sparse our situation, and so in gratitude we do our part.

We remember times in the past when we were helped, times that friends, casual acquaintances, even strangers came to our help when we most needed it. It seemed almost like a miracle at the time, so now we take our turn. We become the miracle for others. We become the vehicle by which the Great Mystery showers gifts upon others, because so many gifts have been showered upon us.

It is a deep honour to witness the Great Mystery unfolding and revealing itself everywhere. So in humbleness we ask, how can I participate? Through prayers of praise and gratitude our senses become heightened so we see and feel the joy of the universe. And from this comes an overwhelming desire to be a servant and vehicle of this glory.

The opened heart easily finds ways to help. Often it is instinctive. Someone slips, your arm goes out. A car is in a ditch, you join the others and push. A colleague at work is depressed, you let him know you care. Already we are kind and loving in many ways, but this can deepen immeasurably. These are only the first few steps on the amazing path to the centre of our heart.

How many times in a crisis situation have you seen

people spontaneously bind together for the common good? A river swells its banks precariously and threatens to spill into town. The town mobilizes. The citizens work all night to avert catastrophe. A call is put out and people respond. They work in unison. Some fill sandbags with gravel, others pack them against the river-banks. Some are working the telephones. Others are cooking meals and still others bring drinks and snacks to the labourers. Total strangers working side by side. And during the crisis there is an exhilaration, a bonding. A feeling of belonging and contributing to something greater than ourselves. Then the problem goes away, people go back to their own lives and everything returns to normal, almost. For something has changed within us. A part of our heart has been touched, opened. We found that we loved helping. It nourished us deeply, and forever we carry within us the tenderness of that event.

Expressing ourselves in such an intimate and unique manner, losing ourselves in service, our oneness is often revealed to us. And here the purity of the experience is felt most deeply. We are lucky, those of us who have had the opportunity to experience such a call and participate in such an event. It is something you never forget.

But if you listen carefully within yourself this very moment, if you open up your heart right now, you will find there is a great call echoing. And you yourself are specifically being called.

The call of the universe to its children is sounding: "Come and participate."

"But I am just one person. I am alone. What can I do?" you might respond.

Alone? Why, there are thousands if not millions of us carrying water and hewing wood in the service of an inner calling. You will see us everywhere if you open your eyes. You too are invited to join, and you will find fellowship here. You need not join any organization, belong to any religion, just follow your heart and do good. This is sufficient. One step at a time is all that is required.

The heart opens slowly and sweetly, like a beautiful flower emerging from a tight, hard bud. One petal at a time until it bursts forth in splendour. So too with us. Do what your heart leads you to do. Follow your heart. Trust your heart. Let your heart lead. Let it bloom. You will be amazed at what happens.

Sometimes when I practice service I do it as an act of worship. I lose myself in adoration and worship of the Great Mystery in which I live and have my being. I am not helping anyone. I am touching the Blessed One. "'For I was hungered and ye fed me. Thirsty and ye gave me drink, sick and ye ministered me, in prison and ye visited me.' And they said amongst themselves, 'Lord when were ye hungry and we fed thee, thirsty and we gave thee drink, sick and we ministered thee, in prison and we visited thee?' And he answered, 'As ye have done unto the least of my brethren ye have done unto me.'"

And so this becomes a living reality to us, not just a spiritual principle. Everyone and everything becomes a manifestation of the Great One. Every act of kindness becomes a prayer and worship. And we see in the eyes of our brothers and sisters the immortal flame of eternity itself.

When I work I try to never feel attached to the results. I

give up the fruits of my work unto the Great Mystery. Whatever good work I may do, I do not claim or expect any praise or benefit. I stand aside and think that I am only a servant obeying my master. A warrior serving my king. Whatever I do, I give up all unto the Mystery and am at rest.

Giving up the fruits of my actions in this way takes away all disappointment and frustration. Sometimes we can get discouraged or disappointed when things don't change or respond the way we think they should. If so we are too involved. Be still. Be at peace. There is a force at work beyond which any of us can understand.

When I strive I feel anxious, not in tune. When I let go, do what I'm called to do and allow things to be what they are, I feel empowered, free, alive. Sometimes I am called to action. Sometimes I am not. This is the way it is. Not all crosses are mine to bear. I have not come to save the world and solve every social problem. It is enough to save myself and maybe make a good hot cup of tea for my fellow brothers and sisters along the way. Anything more is folly and conceit. I listen, obey and then get out of the way.

I do not renounce action. I embrace it and embrace it eagerly if I am so called. What I renounce is the striving. I will do my best and then the universe must look after the rest. For if the truth be known, I can of myself do nothing unless the Great Mystery works through me. And the more I open myself for this to happen, the more it flows and I am blessed.

Let me confess that sometimes when I do my work, there is no 'me' at all, there is only 'it'. How special these times are. And I notice at these times that it strives not,

worries not, concerns itself not with results, exalts itself
not, schemes not, plans not, yet it flows and blesses and
loves and nourishes so perfectly. How easily it works
through me when I am not there. And then I arrive again
with plans, concerns, good intentions, and I catch myself,
step back again and have a good laugh. I feel like writing a
poem.

> *The parched land*
> *Cries, cries.*
> *The trees wither,*
> *The animals,*
> *Walking skin and bones.*
> *Again, the blazing sun*
> *Again, the heat*
> *Again, the vultures feast.*
> *Nothing anyone can do.*
>
> *One day, from nowhere*
> *A cloud appears.*
> *Suddenly the sky is dark.*
> *The rains pour down*
> *The land drinks greedily*
> *Again blooms appear*
> *Again the birds sing sweetly*
> *Again the animals grow fat.*
> *Nothing anyone can do.*

And so it is, has been and will be forevermore. The
Great Mystery has within it rhythms and cycles beyond

what any of us can understand. The tides ebb and flow. The moon grows full and wanes. The affairs of men and nations follow deep rhythms to which we are not privy, and so we allow these things to be, and simply follow our heart wherever it leads us.

I sweep my room clean. I am courteous. My mother and father are getting old, soon they will need care. A friend needs a loan—I give it if I can. Someone is depressed—I listen and care. Someone falls down—I help him up. And if I am called to do more than this I will, but I am never called to strive or worry or concern myself with consequence. A greater one than me looks after these things.

And when I become too full of myself and believe that I am indispensable in any given situation, as sometimes I foolishly do, I simply remind myself that if needed, the universe could raise up a thousand men and women better than me. And so in humbleness I do my part. I am grateful to participate. Honoured to be called upon. Thrilled that I have something to contribute.

I am the branch and the Great Mystery is the tree. I am a vehicle by which the source nourishes and spills out abundantly to its people. Allowing the Holy Source to nourish through me, being its vehicle, I find that I am filled with joy and inner peace. Every cell and atom of my body seems to vibrate and sing. I feel pure, whole, nourished and alive. Such are the blessings of an awakened heart as I have known them, and I have walked just a few steps on this path.

PART IV

The Awakened Dream

♦

ONE

The Warrior and the Sacred Song

And so I saw a thousand warriors
Go forth in their chariots
And in their right hands
A thousand swords unsheathed
Dedicated to the Holy Powers.
And as they rode
A thousand sacred songs filled the air
And great battles were won in this way
And the earth became whole and pure
And all was as it should be.

And the sacred song? What of the sacred song? How is it discovered? How is it awakened? Here a secret is revealed.

Each of us has a gift, a talent to give back to the world. It may be small or large, it does not matter. It is an important part of the Mystery unfolding. The sacred song is our own unique gift, our purpose, and each of us was born to discover and share it with the world.

The sacred song was sown deep within us before we were born, and can only be brought to life when the awakened heart weds the warrior's spirit. Both are necessary. The one without the other will not do.

The awakened heart, like a cosmic mother, longs to birth this gift to the world. It bleeds with the thought that this gift might be lost. That none will hear its melody. For only we can sing our sacred song, no one else. If we do not awaken it, it is lost to the world forever. And so the awakened heart seeks out the warrior spirit, that the two may wed.

We need the warrior's spirit within us. We need to be warriors. The world cries out for warriors. Gentle warriors. Kind and loving warriors but warriors nonetheless. Men and women who are not afraid to follow their vision. To be different. To risk all for the sake of something great. And to do this takes immense bravery.

In Tibetan, the word warrior is translated as one who is brave. To be a warrior is to become brave, but not through arrogance. Rather with humility and trust.

To be a warrior is to greet the day-to-day challenges of our life, feeling secure and confident. To be comfortable in our world. To walk in harmony. To learn to trust our power and the voice within.

The warrior approaches each task with quiet confidence. Confidence because the voice within him is an ally; it guides and directs him. Confidence because the power of the whole universe will come to his aid if he is rightfully aligned. Is this a sacred task? Will it nourish the people? The warrior asks himself these questions every step of the way, and if he can answer yes, then he can call upon all forces of the universe to assist him. All power is at his disposal.

The warrior trains himself to believe this truth absolutely. He leaves nothing to chance. He goes into battle not barefoot and in loincloth but riding a chariot and in full armour. And the chariot is his own beliefs. Warrior beliefs. Spiritual beliefs. Through discipline and training he has created within himself powerful beliefs about himself and his relationship to the Great Mystery, and this is how he rides into battle. Confident and assured.

And in his right hand is a sword unsheathed, dedicated to the holy powers. The sword is the dynamic will, fulfilling the vision of the inner voice. For the warrior fights not just for himself, but for the greatest good of all. He fights to birth the vision and he fights to win. It is his duty to win.

There are many battles to be fought on the spiritual path, and it is within our own temple where some of the fiercest ones take place. There are great victories and bitter defeats within our own selves, and unless we awaken the warrior within us we are sure to be deceived and defeated.

The warrior knows the trickery of the enemy. He does not underestimate the power of laziness, fear, doubt, confusion, feelings of inadequacy and a host of other inner demons to which the polluted waters of our race have given birth. He knows these enemies must be defeated. He stalks them with ingenuity and cunning. Gets to know their ways and habits and then quietly but effectively surmounts them one by one.

True warriorship will take place within us when we shed our weakness and awaken to the fact that we come from a long lineage of great ones, and we agree to take our place amongst them. We accept fully that we are the carriers of the torch of consciousness, with all the responsibilities and powers it bestows. We are the creators of the future.

We are both the seed and the womb through which the future will emerge. And we do not treat this knowledge lightly.

The warrior's spirit exists in one who has dedicated himself to the path. The spirit of the warrior is one of resolve and determination. It is that dynamic element in ourselves that drives through and over all obstacles. It is a commitment to follow the vision whatever the vision may be and wherever it may lead. To be genuine in every moment of our life. To be honest with ourselves. To respect the path we have chosen and to follow it through to completion.

And this is how the sacred songs are birthed. How our destinies are fulfilled. Each of us adding in our own way. Each of us an integral part of the whole. Each of us the Mystery unfolding.

And so the journey continues. The warrior still must seek the kingdom. Two more paths are to be discovered. And so he travels on.

♦

TWO

The Path of Power

The river flows effortlessly
Into the ocean
Losing myself in the Mystery
I find the well is full.

Come, let us drink from the well of living waters. Let us tap into a source of power infinitely more reliable than any you have known before. A source that will never dry. A source that will nourish and uplift you.

All power comes from the Great Mystery. To walk the path of power is simply to increase our realization of this astounding truth. But it must become more to us than a mere concept if we wish to draw upon this source. It must be as real and brilliant to us as the sun at noon. As real as the ground we walk on. No book learning will do here. We must claim our power with authority. And it must be claimed within. It is the realization of who and what we are that gives us power. This we cannot fake or pretend.

It is possible to draw to ourselves whatever we desire. It is possible to become great in whatever our calling. It is possible to be as the mighty ones of old. We can do this because we can draw directly from the great cosmic reservoirs. These are ours to use whenever we align ourselves totally and completely with the source of our being, the source of all power.

And here I encounter a great paradox. I see that the path of power involves becoming less, not more. To the degree that there is less 'me' and more 'it,' to the degree that I, the ego, the human being, decrease and the Great Mystery, the source of all power, increases, to this degree will true and lasting power manifest. When I quiet my mind and remain in stillness and feel this power, even for just a few moments, I feel renewed, expanded, empowered. To do this is to drink from living waters.

Here is the source of my being, I tell myself. Here is the source of all power. And here, too, is my centre, not only my centre but the centre of all centres. And in this holy centre which existed before time itself, I live and move and have my being. Within me flow the living waters. Within me grows the sacred seed. Within me exist the laws and secrets. Within me is the source of all power. Within me lives the Holy Presence. Within me, everything.

A change in one's consciousness is not measured in time but in awareness. No one can tell how long such a thing will take. It can take a year, two years, five years, twenty years for something substantial to happen. It can take six months, two months. It can happen in an instant. These are mysteries no one understands. But this we do know: As our consciousness expands our whole being changes, and we vibrate at a higher frequency. And within these new frequencies inner truths are perceived and felt deeply where before there seemed to be none. Veils are lifted. We see with new eyes, and as these new truths enter into our being they bring with them a new awareness. It is through this deepening of our awareness that the gates of power are opened to us.

"To them that hath, more shall be given; to them that hath not, even what little they have will be taken away."

On the surface this does not seem fair. Surely, to them who have, some should be taken away and given to those who have not. That would seem to be more fair, but that is not what it says. Only upon deeper reflection does the wisdom of this truth reveal itself. For power is like a river flowing and makes no distinction where it flows. One is either aligned with it or one is not. One is either swimming with the current or against it. To recognize the Great Mystery as the source of all things that happen to us, and to align ourselves with it, is to have access to this power. And if we are aligned, we will find that indeed it brings us all we desire.

On the other hand, if we neglect to establish this connection, rely solely on our own means, ignore or forget the powerful forces working within us, then what little we have will be taken away. When we refuse to acknowledge our part in nature, and nature's part in us, we inhibit the flow. We live in darkness. We cut ourselves off. We fight against the current and it is hard and thankless.

When we learn to draw directly from the great cosmic reservoir, we open ourselves up to the ever-present power within us. The amount of energy we receive is limited solely by our capacity for realization; if we can increase our realization we correspondingly increase our intake. This energy is then transmuted within our being into all the different forms of activity that go to make up our life. Every factor in our nature is quickened and intensified. The artist will paint with greater vigour. The writer will write with more power. The athlete will be strengthened. The business person will be more astute. Everything we are will become enhanced and quickened. And all who come in contact with us will feel the effect. For we will become a tributary of the living waters.

Come join me, men and women, and awaken to this power. Brace yourself for the task at hand. Transform your consciousness with new, more powerful beliefs. Wed these new beliefs within you and go to them often. Let them come alive within you. Come live like the mighty ones of old. They are our ancestors. Their blood flows in our blood. This is our destiny.

THREE

♦

Walking the Path of Beauty

Penetrate deep within me
Suck my juices
Let your eyes feast upon me
Let me thrill you with my wonder
Let me intoxicate you with my beauty
Behold, the very ground
you walk upon is holy

It is our sacred duty to awaken beauty in our lives. To behold beauty and cleave it to us. To let it fill our minds and hearts. In this way will we help to purify the consciousness of our race.

The first step on the path of beauty begins when we accept life totally and unconditionally. Learn to think of it as a lover. Like an old friend who has been with us through the ups and downs. Success and failure. Heartaches. Victories. Always there with us and then one day we wake up and realize we are in love. Realize we love it, pain, heartaches and all. We allow life to be what it is. We behold our lover as is. Life becomes our spouse. Our companion. Our friend.

Suddenly we respect it more. What would we do without it? we realize.

When we expect life to always feel good, when we demand that it always please us, bring us the things we desire, we live an illusion. How pitiful. It's neurotic to need to be happy, fulfilled, stimulated every hour of every day. We've become so miserly. We have left no room for pain, confusion, boredom to enter freely into our life. We shun and reject anything unpleasant. Flee from these experiences instead of accepting them as a part of our life. In doing so we have unconsciously rejected life. We wait in anticipation for something different, better than what is happening right now, when in fact all around us the miracle is unfolding. We have impaled ourselves on the sharpened stake of expectation. We wear the thorny crown of desires unfulfilled. We bleed and suffer needlessly over the most inconsequential details of our life. Time to wake up and let go.

For every desire we fulfil, new desires rush to take their place. This was Buddha's great realization. Everything in life is transitory. But if this is the nature of life, our lover, then let us embrace it eagerly. Feel the tenderness and fragility of it all. This makes it all the more precious. For every moment is unique. It can be appreciated only once and only now. If we fail to do this then it is gone and gone forever. Let us kiss our lover each moment. Let us accept it totally. Let go of all that other nonsense. Make your stand. Face life directly and see it now, this very moment. This is our duty.

Everything is perfect in being what it is. When I fully accept this I walk the path of beauty. When I cease my judging, analyzing, criticizing, comparing, I see that all things have their place. Even failure, sickness, misfortune play their part. In the grand scheme of the universe unfolding, all things are as they should be. Not so much as a hair is out of place in this universe. All things are unfolding in their own special way. I have nothing to be concerned with or complain about. On the contrary, I have much to celebrate.

The present moment is always alive and filled with infinite treasures. It contains more than we are capable of receiving. The universe around us is a stupendously complex pattern of events where everything is happening all at once. Life is spilling out at us in abundance. Everywhere. We, however, can only take in one event, one fragment at a time. See the clouds above us in the sky. Listen to the birds singing. The sounds of children playing. Look at the colours all around. Can you see red? Blue? Yellow? Feel the earth we walk upon. Look into my face. Touch my heart. Feel my presence with you. See how the wind blows the branches in the tree. How the flowers bloom. How the insect hums. How the ant crawls. How the night follows the day and the day the night. See the moon. There is more beauty and joy in this very moment than we can ever imagine. And the next moment is just as full, and the moment after that too.

Come, let us read poetry. Listen to music. Make love. Visit a friend. Go on a journey. Cook a meal. Eat and drink heartily. Delight in ourselves. The universe is celebrating. Let us celebrate with it.

Each moment is perfect and complete and whole unto itself. It needs nothing else but for us to come to it. To accept it. To see it. To rejoice in it. A child sees everything as wondrous. A child lives in the moment. Walking the path of beauty means living moment to glorious moment, becoming like a child. Letting everything be new and exciting again.

What is important in a life if not the breeze caressing our skin on a hot summer day? If not the brilliant blooms of a tree in springtime? If not the pleasure of sharing an evening with a good friend. If not gazing at the sky at night with the stars above us. What is important if not these things, and do we not possess them in abundance? Is there ever a moment where we cannot appreciate these gifts spilling out to us in abundance? And if we cannot see this, let us pray that our eyes be opened, for there is much we are missing.

Let us also see the beauty that exists in one another's hearts. Too often we forget this. It is good to remind ourselves that there is much goodness in this world, in the human heart. You will not see it on TV. You will not read about it in the newspapers. But it is there for all to see. Let us acknowledge the fact that for every assault, murder, fraud we hear about, a thousand acts of kindness are performed by ordinary people. We do in fact live in a world where people love and nurture one another.

You don't believe that? You do not see it? Put down your newspapers. Turn off your TVs. Come, take a walk in your own neighbourhood. Open your eyes. Feel people's hearts. There is beauty here. Goodness, generosity, love, concern, fellowship everywhere. See the woman who helps teach English to the new immigrant. Another one who visits the hospital to bring flowers and company to a fellow-worker. Still another who bakes a cake and goes to see her elderly aunt. And another again who helps a friend in time of sorrow. See the man who coaches little league and buys the boys a coke and a burger after the game with money from his own pocket. Another who fixes a friend's car for no remuneration. Still another who organizes a community event. And another working in a soup kitchen to feed the homeless. Are you surprised? Did you not know that the world is a beautiful place to live? Did you not know people's hearts are good? Look in your own heart—is it not good? There are countless others too. Do not be deceived.

If you look for the wonder in the universe it will not take you long to find it. As you do, continually acknowledge it. Praise it. Give thanks for it. Fill your mind with it. It will multiply and pour back upon you a hundredfold. Practice walking the path of beauty until you find that this path of beauty is always under your feet, no matter where you tread.

Practice. One grows with practice. The ballet dancer who moves so effortlessly across the stage practices for hours every day to ensure that her muscles and legs will respond. She makes it look so effortless, yet behind the scenes much work has gone into producing this performance. Did you think the way of the mystic was any different? We must open our eyes and hearts with practice. The long-distance runner practices different exercises from those of the javelin thrower, yet both train rigorously. So too with the one who wishes to awaken to the path of beauty. He or she trains just like the athlete. How? It is simple.

Feed your mind with thoughts of beauty. Practice

seeing it everywhere. Let things thrill you, touch you deeply. Become childlike in your joy and trust. Praise the universe again and again for all its blessings.

Our mind expands and grows with what we feed it. This practice will bear bountiful fruit for us, and, like William Blake, we too will come to see God in a blade of grass and eternity in a grain of sand.

It is easy to think of Blake's words as merely poetic flights of fantasy, yet when the senses become quickened and opened—and they will become quickened and opened—there is more truth here than one could ever imagine. For indeed, when one truly walks the path of beauty everything becomes larger, grander, more alive, and there are moments when we pierce deeply into the mystery, penetrate into its womb, delight ourselves and come up again intoxicated and in awe of what we have seen and experienced.

Walking the path of beauty means worshipping at the temple of ourselves. Celebrating ourselves as beings glorious as the sun. As tender and innocent as new-born babes. As powerful as a raging river. Mysterious. Sacred. Holy. This is who we are.

With practice and careful attention we will see the brilliance of our existence. We will feel it coursing through our veins. Our feet will be firmly planted on the path. Our eyes open. Perceptive. Seeing the divine in all things. Feeling blessed and pure. Flowing. Giddy. Free. Alive to every moment. Taking great gulps of nowness. Beauty everywhere. Intense. Being drawn into the centre of all existence. Gloriously alive. Yes . . . this is the path.

♦

FOUR

The Journey Into Now

Toes in the dirt
Head in the sky
So . . . this is it!

Every day is a journey and the journey itself is home. Here is home. Right where I am, regardless of where I am. Right here in this moment, no matter what this moment is. Whether it is pleasurable or uncomfortable, whether I'm feeling enlightened or confused, happy or depressed—this moment is home. Home sweet home.

It's early morning. I awake, throw water on my face, and there is the journey staring at me. It is always with me. Each day a new part of the mystery unfolds. A new door opens. An old one closes. Each day this journey takes me deeper into unknown territory. I have never been here before. Life flows constantly forward. I flow with it, swept along by the current.

The path of the human being has no end. We are always travelling, becoming something else. We may crave stability, a place to lay our head and be at peace. A place where we 'arrive' and live in contentment and happiness, but this is not to be. As soon as we arrive somewhere it's time to go again. We may experience moments or hours or days of happiness on the journey, but the journey moves on and we must move on with it, always to something new.

I am a nomad. We are all nomads. There is no stability here. No permanence. Nothing to grasp and hold on to. Wherever I put myself down life whirls all around me and marches on relentlessly. I cannot make it stand still. It is not in its nature. It is foolish to try. I cannot make life conform to my expectations.

I can coax it. I can try to direct it in the ways I want it to go. And I do these things and sometimes very successfully. But just when I think I've got life figured out and co-operating with me, off it goes, full of twists and turns, absurd reversals, outrageous surprises, crises, things you could never imagine, and it won't stop. I breathe in and I breathe out. A bird flies by. The sun is going down. Soon the moon will appear. Everything is moving, changing, becoming something else. The very earth below me is dancing in molecular particle activity. And here I am trying to bring stability into my life?

Home is movement, constant movement. If I wish to be comfortable in my home I had best embrace the journey, pack my bags and travel lightly. I can see now that I've been carrying too much baggage. No wonder I have felt weighted down. So I rid myself of excess baggage. I resolve to lose my life in order to find it again. And no sooner do I do this than remarkable things begin to happen. With the smell of the open air and the wind at my back, I discover that I am at the very centre of the universe, always was, always will be. And the pulsating, shimmering, ever-present Now reveals itself to me and becomes my companion.

It is late morning. I've promised a friend that I will pick up a package from the post office for her. Now comes with me. I see an acquaintance on the way. I wave to him and he waves back. The trees look lush today. The mountains are covered in mist.

Letting go. Letting go. Joyously letting go. The eternal breaking into time, becoming my companion. Unspeakable, profound, full of glory as an inward experience. There is another reality here. Ever so subtly it stirs within me. Always there but seldom seen, I let it enter me, swallow me and I become transformed. Now becomes alive, radiant, all encompassing. The Now contains all. Nothing is needed when I lose myself in its presence. Desires, worries, what are these? How feeble. How pitiful. They disappear in shame, scurrying frantically. They know they possess no glory like what is present and unfolding. Even thoughts themselves seem restrained, subdued, timid.

It is mid-afternoon. The sun is shining. I've things to do. Time to go shopping. Now comes with me to the store. Now shops with me. Now helps me choose what items to buy. Driving home Now is not there, or rather I am not there with it. I am thinking, planning what I will be cooking tonight. Friends are coming over. I've promised my wife I will cook. All this is going through my mind as I drive home. I find that Now does not like thinking. It is rarely there when I am thinking.

It's 7 p.m. I am chopping vegetables for tonight's meal, only I am not chopping vegetables. It is chopping vegetables. I am alive in the miracle witnessing this. Now is with me. I hold the carrot in my hand and I see its orange and feel its texture and know it has come from the soil where the sun and earth has nurtured it well. I feel this deeply as I hold the carrot. It is long and I see its longness. I feel its longness. Its longness enters into me. I see the tomato round and red, and the red is tomato red, fully red. I see the grains of the wooden chopping board, feel its texture, watch it flow.

I hear Sylvia laughing and talking with friends in the other room. The guests have arrived, their voices like wind chimes, thrilling me. Outside the kitchen window a tiny branch with red berries. Red like the tomato only more brilliant, deeper, berry red. Small little berries sharing the Now with me and the carrot and the tomato and Sylvia and the voices and the cutting board.

I slice the carrot once and the sound of the knife on the board is the sound of life. It is like a tiny hymn. Complete and full in itself. The carrot slice leaves the carrot effortlessly. The knife handle smooth in my hands. Music is playing. People are laughing. And all this is happening in a fraction of a second. All of it, I am aware. All of it thrilling me.

◆

Losing myself in Now, a fluidity takes hold. A fusion of one hundred million sensations all packed into the instant. The dance of Shiva. Sounds, colours, events, the universe unfolding. Frame by frame it unravels. It is Now that gives it the kiss of life. Makes it all so vivid.

Now puts everything on a pedestal. Worships it. Proclaims it more holy than all. And so it is that each thing reigns in its own way, with its own glory and grandeur. Untouched. Magnificent. Holy. Never have I felt more alive.

I celebrate this day, this moment. Needing nothing. Wanting nothing. Everything contained within myself this very second. Where should I be but here? Who should I be but myself? What time is better than this which is bursting forth in front of me?

And suddenly, all at once, I see it clearly. I see the kingdom clearly. Now I know. The kingdom is here this very instant. The kingdom I have sought so diligently is none other than my own awakened consciousness. I have been at the steps of the kingdom all my life and knew it not.

Oh how subtly the mystery has been hidden. The kingdom contained in every second. Contained in every person and every thing within the second. Searching for it everywhere and finding it not, for how long? And now I see it everywhere.

Our mortal eyes see it not, so preoccupied are we with day-to-day affairs, but spiritual senses, once awakened, fly to it like a bird to a nest, and we are carried along, and suddenly we are in the kingdom. One enters the kingdom not through truths or teachings but moment to moment, surrendering to the Mystery.

Each moment is a holy place. Each moment is my lover. I suck each moment deeply. Know it completely. Drink its essence. Am its witness. All is contained within it. And here I am right in the very centre. Alive. Joyously alive. I am thrilled that so incredible a thing could be happening to me.

Behold, I see the Great Holy One reigning in glory everywhere. The kingdom is within and without. Nowhere is it not. Now that the veil has been lifted, everything is radiant and gloriously alive. To know this is to live in the kingdom forevermore.

◆

FIVE

All and Everything

The secret of your being
is written on every leaf
and every drop of rain
that falls from the sky.
Nowhere can you look
and it is not there.
Open your eyes within
and you will see
that it is true.

Now I see. I am the looking-glass through which all is beheld. And nothing is unholy or defiled unless I make it so.

I am the prism by which all is perceived. I need not change, make myself better or more beautiful—I have merely to behold myself as beautiful and in the prism it will be so. Ugly, it is so. Wondrous, it is so. Unworthy, it is so. All exists and all exists within. And so it has been and will be forevermore.

And so I choose to behold myself and my life through the vision the Great Mystery has shown me. What I have seen and felt in my most exalted states, this I will make mine. I will be like the baker who kneads the yeast within the flour so that the dough will rise and the two become one.

My life will be the table upon which I labour. My experiences will pass through my hands lovingly and expertly, and I will knead and bake a fine bread.

When I have been lifted up and have transcended my normal consciousness, I see that all is glorious, and so this will be my vision. From this palette I will paint my life.

I will behold my life as glorious in sickness as well as in health.

I will behold my life as glorious in failure as well as success.

I will behold my life as glorious in despair and in hope.

I will behold my life as glorious in sadness and happiness.

And this will be my gift. This is my sacred song. To behold the glory and wonder, and to proclaim it loud and clear for all to hear.

I can think of no greater honour than to honour myself. To honour my life. To honour the breath that enters my nostrils. To honour all that my eyes can see and my hands can touch. To honour the ground I walk upon and every person I meet thereupon. I may accomplish no great thing in my life, but if I can accomplish this then I have done well.

Each day will become my miracle, not because of any specific thing that is miraculous. No, simply because I am alive and live with and within my Beloved. Within the Great Mystery I live and move and have my being; this is the miracle.

In prayer and meditation it is there.
While I do the dishes it is there.
Making love to my wife it is there.
Always, always, forever and always there.
In my pain—there.
In my confusion—there.
In my suffering—there.
In my joy—there. Always. Always there.

And so each day becomes a tribute and a prayer and a worship by which the Beloved and I communicate.

To outside eyes nothing is happening. Why tell? It is our secret. No one need know, but within my soul we are together and my heart sings. Always together. Always one. Holy, holy, holy art thou Oh Mysterious One.

And were my life to end. My life to be no more. I would ask only a moment to pay my tribute:

Oh Holy Great One who has created
me and all and everything.
Hear my song. My final song.
Thou hast touched me ever so sweetly.
Thou hast shown me such wonders.
I have walked in forests.
Slept in the open fields
under the stars at night.
I have seen the sun rise and set.
The crescent moon, the full moon.
I have heard the sound of the owl, the hawk, the eagle.
I have seen the ant, the moose
the moth, the whale,

Creatures large and small.
I have seen rainbows and mountains,
I have seen the mist in the early morning.

I have felt the wetness between a woman's legs
Known the pleasure of her moans.
Tasted her sweetness.
I have felt the joy of friendship,
the richness and abandon of love.
I have tasted success and failure.
Loyalty and betrayal, and have learned from it all.
And all of it. All of it from you.
This I now know.
It was your way of loving and delighting me.
Oh how thou hast touched me
Ever so sweetly, deeply, intimately, privately.
What sacred kisses these were
Oh how eager and wondrous your embrace.

Holy, holy, holy thou art, Great Mysterious One
Let every living thing far and wide,
Let the earth and sky, the sun and moon
Hear my words.
I loved you greatly.
And greatly, oh so greatly, didst thou love me.

And this would be my song.

JOHN KEHOE, entrepreneur, writer, philanthropist and social activist, was born in Toronto and now resides in Vancouver, Canada. In 1975, he withdrew to the wooded seclusion of the British Columbia wilderness to spend three years in intensive study and contemplation of the inner workings of the human mind. By borrowing freely from a wide variety of scientific and spiritual sources, and by applying his own shrewd observations and insights, Kehoe was able to forge the first straightforward and successful program for developing mind power. In 1978, he began travelling and teaching people the principles he had formulated, and the phenomenal success of his speaking tours soon grew to literally encompass the globe.

Mind Power was published in 1987 and quickly became an international best-seller, translated and published in a multitude of countries including France, Germany, China and Korea. John's second book, *Money, Success & You*, was published in 1990 and has also been widely acclaimed.

Currently, in addition to annually leading a spiritual wilderness retreat called "Awakening Another Reality," John continues to write and tour, covering a broad range of topics in his lectures and seminars. Although he is well-read in topics as diverse as physics, religion, psychology and shamanism, he credits much of his success to "keeping things simple." His teachings emphasize technique over theory and act as an endorsement of John's strongly held belief that "any system is only as good as the results it produces."

MIND POWER
John Kehoe

Every human being can quickly and efficiently master the essence of mind power. John Kehoe's first book provides the reader with proven means for harnessing inner forces and actively participating in the creative process of achieving your goals. The text covers such techniques as:

- Visualization
- Contemplation
- Prosperity Consciousness
- Intuition
- Beliefs and Imprinting
- Fulfilling Relationships

"A profound study of the human mind."

Le Lundi

MONEY, SUCCESS & YOU
John Kehoe

In *Money, Success & You*, John Kehoe shows that there are powerful, tangible reasons to take control of your own destiny. The book reveals how to gain financial prosperity by learning to shift your focus to those facts and practices that represent proven value in the current information wilderness.

"There is genius, power and magic within us—John Kehoe explains how to awaken it."

Sunday Dominion Times

"With wit and insight, John Kehoe demonstrates that success isn't about hard work but about thinking in original ways."

Successful Salesmanship

AUDIO TAPES BY JOHN KEHOE

The Secret of Happiness
John Kehoe shares with you natural and uncomplicated methods for a full and contented life.

Programming for Prosperity
This tape focuses on methods and techniques to achieve affluence and respect as an individual.

Health and Healing
In this live recording, John Kehoe presents his methods for the attainment and maintenance of vigorous good health.

GUIDED VISUALIZATION AND AFFIRMATION AUDIO TAPES:

In this series of recorded teaching sessions, John Kehoe guides you through simple and proven techniques of visualization and affirmation:

1. *Creating An Abundance of Money*
   Each exercise on this tape works to instill a strong ability to attract money, and to affirm your right to be wealthy.

2. *Incredible Sales Success*
   Techniques to reshape your approach to success and sales, and to recognize the many opportunities that exist around you.

3. *Fit, Slim and Looking Great*
   John Kehoe provides specific exercises to create and
   sustain a good body image.

4. *Healing Yourself*
   Exercises for promoting your own health, and for
   directing your body's natural healing powers.

5. *Attracting A Fabulous Relationship (for women)*
   In relationships, as in everything else, we get exactly
   what we believe we'll get. John Kehoe teaches you to
   revise your expectations and apply proven techniques to
   secure a marvellous relationship.

6. *Attracting A Fabulous Relationship (for men)*
   Learn to recognize and build on your own positive
   qualities, and to begin applying mind power techniques
   to attract the woman you've been waiting for.